Y0-BQX-165

Sibling
Grief

Sibling Grief

✦

Healing after the Death of a Sister or Brother

P. Gill White, PhD

Director, The Sibling Connection

iUniverse, Inc.
New York Lincoln Shanghai

Sibling Grief
Healing after the death of a sister or brother

Copyright © 2006 by P. Gill White

All rights reserved. No part of this book may be used or reproduced by any means, graphic, electronic, or mechanical, including photocopying, recording, taping or by any information storage retrieval system without the written permission of the publisher except in the case of brief quotations embodied in critical articles and reviews.

iUniverse books may be ordered through booksellers or by contacting:

iUniverse
2021 Pine Lake Road, Suite 100
Lincoln, NE 68512
www.iuniverse.com
1-800-Authors (1-800-288-4677)

ISBN-13: 978-0-595-38513-3 (pbk)
ISBN-13: 978-0-595-82894-4 (ebk)
ISBN-10: 0-595-38513-3 (pbk)
ISBN-10: 0-595-82894-9 (ebk)

Printed in the United States of America

For All Surviving Siblings

Contents

Acknowledgements

I want to thank my husband, Granville White, for his unfailing support and help throughout the writing of this book. The book would not have been possible without the website, and I would like to thank my son, Alistair White, for designing the new site and patiently donating his time to it. I'm grateful to my friend, Mary LeTellier, for her compassionate responses to site visitors and to my daughter, Heather White, for listening to the memories. I am grateful to all those who have contributed to what we know about grief and mourning, especially Therese Rando and Joanna Fanos, who encouraged me to write. Special thanks to all the bereaved siblings who have contributed their stories for the making of this book.

Introduction

"Don't tell Mom!" my sister warned. We were planning a vacation during Spring break and she had a pain in her side. She whispered this information to me, swearing me to secrecy, so it wouldn't spoil our trip. A week later, on the day of her thirteenth birthday, she finally told Mom. Linda died four months later from a rare form of cancer called rhabdomyosarcoma. I was fifteen years old.

My parents called us into the living room and told us that everyone had losses, and that talking about it made people sad. They did not know about the healing power of those painful feelings called grief. After the funeral, we moved from Colorado to California, and started over in a new place. My sister's clothes and toys magically disappeared.

Years later, when my first child reached the age of thirteen, my grief returned in full force. I could not find a counselor who understood about sibling loss. I heard statements like, "You should be over that by now!" I spent the next several years figuring out what was happening to me, went back to college, and became a counselor myself. On the anniversary of my sister's birthday, ten years ago, I posted my first hesitant website to the Internet. It is called the Sibling Connection, a place where bereaved siblings can find validation for their feelings, tell their stories, and meet others like them.

The response has been overwhelming. Many of the thousands of visitors write to thank me for the site. Some have become good friends. The purpose of this book is to share what I have learned on this journey, both from my own education and clinical work with bereaved siblings, and from the Sibling Connection.

I finally found a place where I could talk about what happened during those four months of my sister's illness.

My sister did not know that she was dying and we were not supposed to tell her. But one dark night, as I sat in a chair, leaning on her hospital bed, I thought she was asleep. Out of the silence, she began to speak.

"Promise me you will keep singing," she said quietly. "Promise me you will go to college."

"I will," I answered. "I promise."

At that moment, I had the sensation that I was sitting on the bank of a river and she was lying in a boat, moving with the current. As her boat passed by, I reached over and grabbed the dreams—our childhood dreams of growing up together, singing together, going to college, becoming teachers, traveling, getting married, and settling down with six children each and living next door to each other—I knelt on the river bank in my imagination, clutching an armload of dreams, like laundry out of the dryer, and watched her float away.

You don't ask people to make promises like that unless you already know you are going to die.

I have learned that we never really get over the loss of a brother or sister.

This book is for all bereaved siblings of any age, and for parents who want to help their surviving children. There are chapters on the specifics of losing a brother or sister during childhood, adolescence, and adulthood, but they apply to us all. In some ways our siblings never age. If they die when we are adults, we feel the loss of the child they once were. If they die when we are children, we grow up and feel the loss of the adult they would have become.

There has been a great deal of research on sibling loss, described in academic literature that is sometimes difficult to read. My hope is that this book will reach a wider audience and make the information garnered from research available to everyone. The chapter on the five healing tasks represents wisdom based on research and on meeting with hundreds of bereaved siblings in my office and online. There is a section about the long-term effects of sibling loss, one on creativity, and one about the ongoing connections we keep with our lost siblings, including the dream patterns that reflect healing. There are poems and stories from other cultures. The final chapter is about bibliotherapy, or the use of books to help us heal. It includes a detailed outline for how to use bibliotherapy, as well as a book list.

After you read this book, I welcome you to visit the Sibling Connection online. Our vision is that all bereaved siblings will receive the support they need. Our mission is to provide resources to grieving siblings through counseling, education, research, writing, and by raising public awareness of the profound impact of sibling loss.

1

Death of a Sibling During Infancy or Childhood

o o o o o o o o o o o o o o o o o o o o o o o o o o o o o o o o o o o

A simple child, that lightly draws its breath,
and feels its life in every limb,
What should it know of death?

—Bereaved parent, Wm Wordsworth: We Are Seven

This chapter is for everyone—for adults who lost a sibling when they themselves were children, for all bereaved siblings, and for parents who have lost a child and want to learn how to help their surviving children. Throughout this book, I refer to the grieving siblings as survivors.

The early death of a brother or sister profoundly changes the lives of surviving siblings. They hurt, but don't fully understand; they feel rejected and are afraid they are to blame. They fear that they, or someone else they love, might die next. Research shows that such a major loss adversely affects surviving children's health, behavior, schoolwork, self-esteem, and development.

Surviving siblings may be troubled throughout life by a vulnerability to loss and painful upsurges of grief at meaningful times, such as their sibling's birthday or day their sibling died. To defend against loss, they may try to control the people around them and fear loving again. They may develop distorted beliefs about hospitals, doctors, and illness. In the absence of age appropriate information, they create childlike myths to explain what happened, and make up rules to follow in order to avoid further devastation. Such naïve rules for living may follow them permanently.

Many survivor siblings are troubled by guilt due to the ambivalent nature of the sibling relationship. Upon the death of the brother or sister, they remember forcibly all the fights and name-calling, seeing themselves in memory as the bad child and the dead sibling as the good one. This split in self-concept results in the feeling that they are not good enough.

Age, Development, and Attachment

The impact of sibling loss depends in part on the survivor's age, developmental level, and their "attachment style". In the first year of life, when babies are developing a sense of trust, the loss of a sibling means also a loss of crucial time with primary caregivers, who are spending time away from home on hospital visits, their own grief, perhaps even court appearances. School age children are developing a sense of accomplishment and beginning to bond with their peer group. This developmental stage requires ample opportunity for them to explore the world and spend time with friends, opportunities that may be curtailed due to a sibling's illness and death, leaving the child feeling isolated and different from peers.

The way in which we form attachments or connections with loved ones also impacts the severity of the grief response. Psychologist John Bowlby theorized that individuals who learn to trust have a secure attachment style—in other words, they have a deep felt sense of being valued and deserving of care, support, and affection. Those who do not learn to trust because of inconsistent parenting, abuse, neglect, or lack of attunement, form an anxious attachment style. These individuals are fearful and anxious, feel unappreciated and misunderstood, lack confidence, and may worry about others taking advantage of them. Sadly, there is yet a third attachment style, which Bowlby called avoidant or detached. This occurs when the infant learns that its cries will not get a response at all and so does not become attached to others.

Once an individual forms an attachment style, it typically does not change throughout life, and this is why it is so significant when the death of a sibling disrupts the household. The grief does eventually abate, but attachment styles go on for a lifetime.

Infants who lose a sibling may experience a rift in their ability to trust, and thus do not form a secure attachment style. During the first years of life, these young ones depend entirely upon others to meet their daily needs. When responsive caregivers consistently meet their need for food, comfort, and affection, they learn to trust both people and the world in general. If, however, parents do not respond to their child's cries, or trauma occurs, they may not learn to trust. This negative outcome sets the stage for a lifetime of pessimism, as the baby grows into a person who believes the world is basically unsafe. The roots of mental illness in adults sometimes reach back into this phase of development.

This is not to say that every infant who loses a sibling will develop mistrust. In most families, grandparents or other relatives or friends would most likely step in to maintain the infant's routine and feeding schedules. This is all to the good. But the fact that one of the siblings is permanently gone might make the infant fearful and anxious, and erode the consistent care that is so important in developing that all-important feeling of security.

Understanding Death

A child's experience of losing a sibling depends also on their understanding of death and the way that they grieve. These age ranges are approximate, and you (when you were a child) or your child (if you are a parent reading this) may have a broader understanding than those described here.

Toddlers

Toddlers think of death as temporary and reversible. They think in concrete terms (what they can see or touch) and may not comprehend why their brother or sister is in a coffin, and why they can't go see them at the hospital the day after the funeral. When I told my four-year-old sister, Barb, that Linda had died and gone to Heaven, she replied, "We can still write letters to her, can't we?"

This lack of understanding does not prevent them from absorbing the sadness and anxiety around them, so toddlers grieving the loss of a sibling sometimes regress to an earlier stage of development, for example, wetting the bed after they had already become toilet trained, or sucking their thumb, and on rare occasions, becoming mute for a period of time. Children in these younger age groups may have thought about an older sibling as a parent figure who took care of them, and wonder who will take care of them now that the brother or sister is gone.

In some ways, infants and toddlers suffer more than any other age group who lose a sibling. That is because they must now live a lifetime in a family which may have become dysfunctional after the death. We know, for example, that some couples divorce after losing a child, which creates another separation. We know that some parents who lose one child are likely to be overprotective of their remaining children. We know that some parents and siblings may respond to the loss by choosing not to love again, and not risk loving the bereaved infant or toddler. Some parents may actually verbalize their belief that the youngest child should have been the one to die since they didn't know it that well.

Children age 6-8

These children know more about death—they have seen dead birds and bugs, seen people die on television, and heard it talked about. They think of death as a scary thing that they can hide from, by hiding under the bed, for example. They say things like "When your hair gets white, you die, right?" Parents may mistakenly assume that their child understands more at this age than they actually do. For that reason, it helps to be especially clear when communicating to them what is going on.

In this age group, children associate death with ghosts and skeletons. They know what it is, but not how it will affect them personally. They may ask questions about the death over and over. It is as if they have to learn the lesson of death many times for it to sink in.

At these young ages, children engage in what is called "magical" thinking. They may believe, for example, that their anger can kill, and that they cause the events surrounding them. They are still the center of their own universe and may take the blame for the death. Adults bereaved in childhood have often suffered for years, believing that they were responsible for their sibling's death.

Children ages 9-13

Children change at sometime around nine years to a more realistic understanding of death. They know that it cannot be reversed, that it is permanent, and that everyone dies.

Like the younger groups, these children do not behave like adults when they lose a loved one—instead they may act out, or simply act as if nothing happened at all. They may fall asleep or want to go outside and play when everyone else is mourning. Again, they are dealing with reality in their own way, a way that is associated more with their age than the amount of love they had for the deceased.

When a child first experiences a loss, they are just beginning to learn, on a day-to-day basis, what exactly loss feels like and what it means.

In later life, this group often feels guilty about how they acted during the time surrounding the death. Some, for example, had not been able to tolerate the physical pain of their sibling and dealt with this by avoiding them. As adults, they regret not spending time with their brother or sister immediately prior to their death, blaming themselves for not knowing that it was their last chance. Even decades later, these actions continue to cause them intense remorse and emotional pain.

As children, we did the best we could with our limited understanding. If we continue to have difficulty with guilt and remorse about such issues, we can go and look at a child who is now the age we were when our sibling died. Don't they look young and innocent? Wouldn't we be able to forgive that child? It helps to share our feelings openly with a supportive friend or family member to get them out into the open. When someone else can accept us in spite of what we did or didn't do when our siblings were dying, it will help us to accept ourselves.

How Children Grieve

It is crucial for adults to learn how children grieve. Research shows that bereaved children (and teens) often "act out" their feelings by misbehaving and trying to get attention. They hurt inside and are seeking those critical attachment behaviors (eye contact, touching, clinging, staying near the parent) that will give them comfort. Parents and others might get mad at the child because they are behaving this way, but in reality, this IS the child's way of mourning.

Many adults look back on the way they behaved when their sibling was dying, and suffer more from guilt about their misbehavior than they do from any other aspect of the loss. When adults shame or belittle siblings for their behavior, survivors feel inadequate and of little value, a heavy burden for a young child who is already grieving.

Siblings of all ages sometimes feel jealous of the attention given a brother or sister who is sick for a period prior to death, and then feel guilty about having been jealous. Adults who are looking back at their experience need to know that these feelings of jealousy are normal. We cannot judge our childhood selves with the wisdom garnered from an adult lifetime. We need to forgive ourselves.

LifeSpace

Why don't all of the surviving children grieve in the same way?

The loss of a sibling affects each person in the family uniquely, because each relationship is different. Therefore, no two individuals from the same family have the same experience of loss. Some of the factors that influence the nature and intensity of sibling grief are birth order, the personality of the survivor, the psychological health of the family prior to the loss, and how the family handles the loss.

Perhaps the most significant factor that predicts how the surviving sibling's life will be impacted by the loss is that of life space. Life space refers to the amount of time and activities shared with the deceased. Siblings who sleep in the same bed, play together, have the same friends, and spend most of their leisure time together share a great deal of life space. It is as difficult to separate siblings who shared a great deal of life space, as it is to take the yeast out of a loaf of bread without destroying the loaf. There is no separate identity in such cases. We have to learn who we are all over again.

Reactions in the Family—Seven Bereaved Children

As stated earlier, when young children experience the death of a brother or sister, they suffer not only the actual loss, but also a lifetime of living in a family whose response to the loss adds further difficulties.

Researchers have identified seven distinct kinds of survivor siblings, which represent various responses to loss. These are: the haunted child, the over-protected child, the replacement child, the lap child, the lonely child, the later-born child, and the scapegoat.

1. The Haunted Child—Researchers Krell and Rabkin talk about the "haunted child" who lives in families where none of the members talk about what happened. In this case, the survivor sibling is haunted by the knowledge of the death, but cannot speak up to ask about it.

2. The Overprotected Child—Other parents may treat survivor siblings as if they are incredibly precious, and over-protect them in an attempt to prevent another loss. Such treatment may interfere with the child's growth in autonomy.

Also, this treatment may go hand in hand with a subtle form of rejection, because the parent fears getting too close and being hurt again.

3. The Lap Child—In my own clinical work, I have seen a similar phenomenon, the lap child, where an infant or young child, whose sibling is sick for a long time prior to the death, is kept close to his or her mother, because it's easier for the mother, rather than allowing the child to explore and try new activities. The lap child may learn to be passive and helpless because they haven't had opportunities to explore the world.

4. The Replacement Child—The replacement child phenomenon includes three special situations. First, it refers to a child born after the death who is treated as if he or she were the reincarnation of the deceased. In rare cases, this child is even given the same name. This child's identity blurs with that of the deceased, which creates significant difficulties throughout life. A replacement child can also be a child who is adopted or fostered by the family after the death of one of the children. Finally, the replacement child may refer to a surviving sibling who responds by acting like the one who died, as if they are trying to replace the lost brother or sister.

5. The Lonely Child—The lonely child is essentially neglected, due to unavoidable circumstances, such as parental separation and divorce after the death. Sometimes growing up in a single-parent family, perhaps even being the only child left in the family, this child spends much of his or her time alone after school. Pets can be a lifeline for such children.

6. Later-born Children—Children born into a family where the death of one child already occurred experience a variety of emotions. Some feel shut out because the others knew the deceased and they did not. Others feel that the deceased sibling is a real person, one who would have taken their side in arguments had they lived. Later-born children may talk about their sibling as a guardian angel who watches over them, while others blame the deceased for making their parents sad. Some later-born children wonder about their sibling well in to adulthood, and regret the lost opportunity for relationship.

7. The Scapegoat Child—Kay Tooley writes about the "scapegoat" child and describes the phenomenon where one of the survivor siblings is chosen to be the target for a parent's hostility, hostility derived from that parent's own guilt about the death.

What all of this means is that bereaved siblings are subject to further problems depending on how the loss is handled by the family. Having other brothers and sisters at home can help to mitigate these responses.

How parents can help

Parents have a devastating burden placed upon them when they lose a child. They can, however, reduce the burden for their remaining children by the way in which they respond.

This section provides suggestions for parents who are dealing with the survivor siblings. If you are an adult reading this about your own bereavement experience, I recommend that you read each of these suggestions and explore your thoughts and memories about how it was handled in your family. Once we acknowledge and validate our memories and feelings, it becomes easier to forgive others and ourselves.

- Consider your children's feelings. You may be saying, "Why did Johnny have to die?" but they may *hear* you saying, "Why couldn't one of the other kids have died instead?"

- Tell them it was not their fault. They may jump to the conclusion that, because their brother caught a cold from them last year, that they are now responsible for the death. They may have wished the sibling dead at some time during a fight, and now think their wish came true.

- Communicate clearly in age appropriate language what is going on. A three-year-old won't understand that his sister died from complications following surgery, but will understand that her body stopped working. Use specific language, rather than euphemisms. If you tell a child "We lost Billy," he or she may be confused and panicky until you find him.

- Reassure children that they are not going to die and neither are you. Be patient with their repeated inquiries about this.

- When possible, maintain normal household structure with regular meals and bedtimes. Structure helps to keep anxiety in check.

- Let your children see you grieve—don't hide in the bedroom and cry alone. You may be grieving in the bedroom with the door closed, but the other children interpret your behavior as you not wanting to be around them.

- Comfort them with lots of hugs and physical touch.

- Make time to spend alone with each of your children. Tell them you are glad they are with you, glad they are part of the family, and how proud you are of them. If you don't have much time, think of quality, rather than quantity. Even a single experience of alone time with a parent, when they really feel seen and heard, can be held in the heart for a lifetime, to be brought out again and again, when it is needed.

- Get the support and help you need for your grief so that you can be there for the surviving children. When your children feel that you will never be able to focus on them again, they will become angry with you and the one who died. In their hearts they are asking: Do I have to die to get any attention around here?

- If they are struggling, seek out programs for bereaved children. You are the gatekeeper—they cannot find help for themselves.

- Allow them to choose a special item of their sibling's to keep as a linking object.

- Help them to create a store of memories (described later in the book), such as a memory box or scrapbook while their memories are still fresh. If you don't feel well enough to do this with your child, ask a friend to help out. In later years, your children will thank you for this.

Gifts for a lifetime

Parents are often unaware of the power they hold within their families. In particular, any activity that a parent shares happily with a child becomes saturated with love. Long after you are gone, your child will engage in the activity and feel once again the love you shared.

Parents who instill a love of nature by spending time with children out of doors, in visits to parks, camping, hiking, or picnicking give their child a precious gift. In later years, when the now-grown child suffers a blow and is broken hearted, he or she can turn to nature for comfort and still feel loved. Parents who teach their children about the value of exercise, by walking or biking with them, playing ball with them, and supporting their sports events, also give a gift that lasts a lifetime, since exercise is one of the most significant methods of reducing anxiety. As adults under stress, they will be able to go for a long walk and not only feel better from the walk, but also feel your approval, which goes a long way towards reducing stress. A love for reading, for pets, for the environment, for cooking, an interest in history, cycling, boating, crafts, woodworking, or building cars—any activity can be the vehicle to carry love to the next generation.

2

Death of a Sibling as an Adolescent or College Student

o o o o o o o o o o o o o o o o o o o o o o o o o o o o o o o o o o o o

You think, perhaps, that you will live forever,
For death, still out of sight, is out of mind.

—*Nicholas Gordon*

Farewell to Childhood

Adolescence has been described as the "farewell to childhood", when a young person lets go of his or her childhood, grieves its loss, and begins to move into adulthood. Loss of a sibling during this period intensifies the issues related to the normal tasks of adolescence.

Adolescents are capable of an adult understanding of death, but the way in which they grieve is related to both children and adults. Since they have the capacity to think like adults, adolescents may suffer more from the effects of loss than children, who are protected somewhat by their concrete or magical way of thinking.

The main difference between the grief of adults and that of adolescents is the amount of power or autonomy the individual holds. Most adults can reach out for the help they need through counseling, church, synagogue, or support groups. Adolescents, however, need their parents' permission and help in order to seek the same kind of support. Parents may be so caught up in their own grief, that they cannot even see the pain of their children. Other parents may see the pain,

15

but do not want outsiders to get too close to their family for fear they will be criticized.

Awareness of the reality of death and subsequent sense of vulnerability shakes the very foundation of the adolescent's still fragile identity. Midway between the two domains of childhood and adulthood, adolescents have a strong drive towards autonomy and independence, and they may resent being over-protected by parents.

Not only have they lost a beloved brother or sister, but also they are faced with the reality that they too will die someday. So, they desperately want to regress to get the needed support. This conflict is critical to understanding the unique experience of grieving teenagers who have lost a sibling.

Although adolescents know and understand mentally the reality of death, what makes grieving particularly troublesome at this age is the conflict in their feelings. They are just at the point when they are moving away from their families emotionally in the normal separation/individuation process we all go through to form a unique identity. They often appear to know everything, and feel that nothing bad can happen to them.

At best, this conflict in an adolescent's feelings is resolved by going to their peers for support. They can get support from their peers without having to regress to what seems to them as a childlike state when they get support from parents. However, many surviving siblings have told me that they could not go to their peers because they felt so different from them.

At the worst, their grief is pushed underground, and may result in disorders of conduct, such as the use of drugs and alcohol, poor school performance, loneliness, a tendency to withdraw from relationships, low self-esteem, depression, and difficulty in making long-term commitments.

The healthy resolution of grief depends on a number of factors. First is the nature of the relationship with the sibling prior to death, and the relationship with the parents and other surviving siblings. When the family is secure, and the children feel their home offers a comfortable place for them to retreat to when they are hurt, they will probably fare better after the loss of a family member.

Being given timely and accurate information about the sibling's illness or circumstances surrounding the accident is crucial. Some siblings have spent years in wondering about the details of what happened to their sibling because the parents did not want to talk about it. Others have suffered needlessly because parents tried to hide the facts surrounding the death. Young people need to ask questions and have an adult answer and explain what they need to know. They should be given the opportunity to attend or even participate in the funeral. They need to be reassured about the continuing security within the family, although one of their members has died.

College Age Siblings

The loss of a brother or sister is particularly difficult for college students, since it happens at a time that already stresses many individuals beyond their capacity to cope. Returning to college after a funeral, students may experience a sense of unreality, or a feeling of living in a surreal world. If bereaved students are going to continue with studies, they must deal with their grief process in this sometimes less structured environment, and it may be especially challenging for them to obtain the necessary support.

Long periods of unstructured time, such as long weekends or Sunday afternoons, create an environment in which depression thrives. External structure helps to keep emotions in check. It is not unusual to experience periods of feeling down or lonely in college under normal circumstances, 'the college blues'. This sounds like we're talking about sadness and depression, but anxiety and stress also play a part.

There are a variety of reasons why college students are already feeling low. The role once held in high school disappears, once-popular students are now unknown, and there is a stressful period of reorganization and finding a new niche in a new environment. Losing a sibling on top of all this is challenging indeed.

Loneliness at home or college

Of all the effects described in research on bereaved siblings in this age range, the most common is a sense of feeling different from others. There is nearly always some loneliness associated with grief. Each relationship is entirely unique. Each person within the family will have lost a different relationship, even though it was the same person who died. Therefore, no one else can possibly know exactly what our grief is about and what we lost.

Sometimes bereaved siblings search and search for someone who understands, but the sad fact is that no one can completely understand. During a period of grief we truly learn the meaning of being alone.

Students come to college with various mechanisms for "self-soothing", a term which describes how we cheer ourselves up when we feel down or calm ourselves down when we feel anxious. Typical self-soothing mechanisms range along a spectrum from self-talk, physical activity, talking to a friend, eating, sleeping, going online, instant messaging, and playing games—all the way to drinking and using drugs, which may be unconscious attempts to self-medicate emotional pain.

We thrive best when surrounded by a community of supportive people among whom we can grow and develop. But even in such a setting, we can still be lonely if we are wearing a mask, pretending to be someone we are not, or pretending to be happy when we are torn up inside. Masks also keep out the good feelings that come our way from others. Clearly, it is crucial to find someone to talk to so you can let down your mask and share your true feelings.

Trauma

If you were in high school or college at the time of a sibling's death, it is statistically likely that your sibling died in an accident or from suicide. The psychic trauma following a sudden and unexpected event exceeds the capacity of the individual's coping skills and psychological defenses, so that they become temporarily helpless. This may result in distorted memories, lack of trust, a pessimistic attitude towards life, and low self-esteem. The trauma itself gets in the way of the successful resolution of the grief. When survivors think about the deceased sibling, they become 'stuck' at the traumatic event that caused the death and can't remember other, happier times. Such cases may result in complicated grief that, over time, leads to an anxiety disorder or depression.

Recovery from trauma involves working through the pain, and articulating thoughts and feelings about the loss to a trusted person. While this long process is going on, we can gain strength by working to increase our self-esteem. Each step that we take towards becoming our best self will create a corresponding rise in self-esteem. We will then be strong enough to handle another 'piece' of our grief. Traumatic grief must be dealt with bit by bit, not all at once.

What helps and hurts

Research in various studies, including one carried out at the Sibling Connection, shows there is help for bereaved siblings. When asked about what helped them to survive this terrible loss, adolescent survivors list the following:

- Writing about it, and writing letters to the one who died (even if this is just a mental letter, not actually written down) is helpful.
- Having faith in a higher power
- Parents who care about you
- Professional counseling
- Having other siblings to be with you
- Volunteering time at shelters during the holidays
- Playing musical instruments,
- Exercise
- Keeping busy
- Expressing emotion
- Writing poetry
- Talking with caring others
- Journaling
- Online chatting
- Making photo albums and scrapbooks
- Painting
- Creating memorial websites
- Visiting the Sibling Connection

And the following list is what hurts:

- The grief of parents, when that grief made them feel as if the parent wished the surviving sibling had died instead, for example, when parents make comments like "I have nothing to live for now".

- Being sent to stay with relatives while parents recovered
- Not being told the truth about the death, and being kept in the dark about significant issues related to the death
- When people ask how their parents are doing, but do not ask how they are doing.
- When parents compare them negatively to the deceased sibling.

Sibling rivalry beyond the grave

The rivalry once experienced between siblings does not end with death. Parents may expect them to include the deceased sibling in all of their special events, perhaps by having a photograph or flowers on display at their wedding, for example. Not every bereaved sibling will wish to remember the death at happy times, and some will feel that they have to compete with their sibling once again. Families tend to idealize deceased children. It can be extremely difficult for surviving siblings to measure up to this ideal.

The Transformative Power of Grief

People change in significant ways after the death of a sibling, since we do have the capacity to learn from our experiences, whether they are positive or negative. Many adolescents find that their experience with death has taught them a great deal about life. In spite of the unfairness and devastation associated with the loss of a brother or sister during adolescence, the pain and guilt often leave wisdom and love in their wake. Survivors appreciate life and relationships more, feel closer to God, and are able to listen to and be with others who are grieving.

Some bereaved adolescents go on to become adults who work in the area of counseling, research on sibling loss, ministry, and social work. Finding ways to make sense of this loss motivates some adolescents to become adults who make significant contributions in the realm of emotional healing.

Returning to School

Here are some ideas to help you when you return to school after the loss of a sibling:

- Seek out and use whatever resources are available at your school, such as counseling or support groups.

- Talk to your teachers or professors if you need to make changes in your schedule, or need additional help because of a lack of concentration.

- If you find yourself "self-medicating" with alcohol and drugs, get help! Talk to your school counselor, campus chaplain, or doctor.

- Before sharing the experience of your sibling's death at school, consider how much the other person cares about you. While those who care and have experienced loss themselves may be helpful and comforting, others may alienate you, since they don't know what to say or do.

- If necessary, be proactive with your grief. Find time during the day or week to deliberately confront it, and find appropriate others to be with you at this time. Since many students have unrealistic ideas about how long it takes to recover from a loss, the most appropriate help at this time might have to be a professional caregiver.

- Reduce your stress level by not taking on too many demanding tasks.

- As I stated elsewhere, learn about the grief process and about sibling loss. This cognitive understanding will help to support you when your feelings seem uncontrollable.

- If possible, talk to other bereaved students—your school or college counselor may be able to help you find them. This will help you feel less alone.

- Don't measure your grief by any one else's standard. We all have our own unique way of dealing with loss, and each loss is different. Don't worry about whether you are doing it "the right way".

- Other students and even teachers and professors may not know the best way to approach you after your loss. Be patient with them.

Final note—the best gift

If you lost a sibling during this period of life, you need to know that it is normal for you to still want to have fun with your friends and enjoy life. You don't have to feel guilty for wanting to laugh and be with people your own age. Some survivors feel they don't have the right to have a normal life, but that is not true. Being happy and glad to be alive does not mean that you have forgotten your sibling. The best gift you can give your brother or sister is to continue to live life to the fullest.

3

Death of an Adult Sibling

○ ○

The ringing phone still echoes in memory,
I didn't get a chance to say good-bye.

—Bereaved sibling, Lenora McIntyre

Disenfranchised Grief

After the death of a sibling, adult survivors often feel abandoned by society. While sympathy flows to their parents or their sibling's spouse and children, brothers and sisters are expected to recover quickly. This is one of the reasons why adult sibling loss falls into the category of "disenfranchised grief", where someone feels they don't have the right to grieve. Lack of support makes it difficult to resolve the grief so survivors often struggle for years with a low-grade depression.

Adult siblings, who have left home and perhaps have families of their own, form a special category of sibling loss that is sometimes overlooked. On the one hand, adults feel towards their sibling as if they are still children together no matter what age they are now. When a sibling dies, a piece of childhood goes too. On the other hand, they are truly adult, feeling the full force of grief. Adults have had a lifetime of memories and connections which are torn apart by the loss.

Putting Grief on Hold

The pattern or trajectory of grief for many bereaved siblings—regardless of age—often includes a period of delayed mourning. For teenagers, the delay may come about because the individuation process takes precedence over their grief. With adults, however, the delay is more likely to be caused by an attempt to help others, the desire not to upset others, a fear of emotion, or a desire to get back to work.

Often living at a distance from the one who died, adult siblings may hide their emotions and attempt to go about their everyday life as soon as they return from the funeral. People around them, not personally acquainted with their deceased brother or sister, may support them initially but subtly reject them if the grief goes on too long. Those who have never experienced loss have unrealistic ideas about how long it takes.

The desire to protect someone else also complicates the grief process for adult siblings. The focus on being strong for someone else—perhaps their parents, a spouse, or their own children—helps put the grief process on hold, which can be carried too far. It becomes counter productive when bereaved siblings project their sad feelings onto others, and then take care of those others. The grief is still there, inside. This compulsive caregiving focuses so much energy outside that the grieving person may become empty inside and clinically depressed.

To help resolve this compulsive caregiving, surviving siblings need to confront their own sadness and pain, own it, and feel it deeply. This is the way to grow through the grief. They may need to talk about every detail of the death, and express the associated feelings over and over again. Surviving adult siblings need to give themselves permission to grieve in a place that feels safe to them, and take time to deal with their own sense of loss.

How an individual integrates the loss of a sibling will impact his or her entire life. Clearly it is not only the death of the sibling, but the manner in which their grief is handled that shapes the surviving sibling's future. All too often, the grieving individual buries his or her feelings in order to achieve acceptance from peers and family members. We all need acceptance and, at the same time, need validation for our feelings.

We have choices about how to deal with the way others communicate with us during this period of bereavement. We can resist any emotional intimidation, thus empowering our sense of self, and maintaining our integrity. If significant others fail to support us, we may begin to think they are not as significant as we thought. We can attempt to teach them how to respond to our feelings if the relationship is important enough, or we can look elsewhere for validation

People who have never experienced this loss do not understand how devastating is the death of a sibling—but they are not deliberately being cruel by failing to comprehend the magnitude of our grief. It is up to us to communicate with others and teach them about this profound loss. If our goal is to simply to please others, we may end up hiding our grief and perpetuating the common misunderstanding that sibling loss is insignificant.

Adults have several major challenges to face after the death of a brother or sister:

Seeking a New Identity

Sibling lives are intertwined much like the threads of a fabric. They make up part of who we are. Bereaved adult siblings often experience a profound sense of identity confusion, which may lead to their becoming isolated or depressed. Most of us are familiar with the identity crisis that occurs at adolescence, when teens struggle with the changes that puberty brings. An identity crisis, however, is not limited to adolescents and is common during bereavement.

The term "identity" refers to our sense of self that remains the same over time. We form our identity against a background that includes all of our family members. There is a part of us who relates to Mom, to Dad, and to each brother and sister. When our sibling dies, the part of us that related to the sibling seems to die too, creating a rift in the unbroken wholeness that we called our "Self". The sense of self that once carried us so easily from day to day is shaken to the core. It takes time and healing to create a new identity.

The more of our life that we shared with our sibling, the more seems to be missing. It might feel like we lost so much of ourselves that we can hardly go on living without them. We might feel like just a shell of a person. Some surviving siblings considered their unmarried brother or sister part of their nuclear family, because they spent time together at holidays and saw each other on a regular basis. For those who are widowed, the sibling who died may have seemed like a significant other. The lost sibling may have been the only part left of their deceased parents.

When a brother or sister dies, the way we see ourselves within the family changes, even though we are grown and no longer living in our parents' home.

Some survivors go from being a sister or brother to being an "only child". Some change from being a "twin" to an "only". Some move from "middle child" to "oldest child". A death often requires us to take on new roles once filled by, or at least, shared with, the sibling who died, such as caring for aging parents. Struggling with these changes, we feel helpless, frustrated, and fearful.

This change within the family is critical to the way in which siblings heal. How we develop in relationship to our siblings relates to the concept of birth order. The first-born child develops certain specific characteristics and talents. The children born later will most likely choose different characteristics to develop in order to distinguish themselves from one another.

Siblings support each other by their differences. The strength and talent of one is shared by all. When one of the siblings dies, that strength is lost, and the survivor's identity changed. It takes times to learn how to live life again. We have to grow within ourselves the parts once carried by our brothers and sisters. We don't "get over" this as much as "grow through" it.

We hear so much about sibling rivalry that sometimes we forget the depth of sibling closeness. Comments from bereaved siblings show their attempt to describe the diverse nature of the sibling relationship, the feelings of closeness, and what their sibling meant to them.

"We were always together so people called us 'right and left'."

"We were like peas in a pod."

"He was my guardian, he watched over me, and kept me out of trouble."

"He was like my own child, because we were twelve years apart. I carried him around and babysat him."

"She was my best friend, not just my sister."

"We were like two sides of one coin."

"He was my mentor, my guide."

"She was the best part of me."

"We called each other every day, no matter how far apart we lived.

"I wanted to be like him."

"She looked up to me and kept me motivated."

These comments emphasize a special feature of sibling relationships. Sometimes we look up to our siblings, but at other times, they look up to us. And yet, in some ways, we are on an equal level. This richness in the relationship helps fill our need to admire and be admired, and to have a person around who is just like us.

We have lost not only this rich relationship with our siblings, but also the part they would have played in our future. We go on to marry, have children, buy a house, succeed or fail, and each event underlines the terrible reality that our brother or sister is not there. Forever after, significant events, no matter how wonderful, have a bittersweet flavor.

Coping with Marital and Family Changes

People who have not experienced grief may believe that when someone dies, they simply grieve, recover, and then move on with life. Unfortunately, it is not so clear and simple. The initial loss of a brother or sister leaves ripples of loss extending well beyond what most people expect. One of the major causes of conflict between family members, especially that between husband and wife, is grief. To understand why, and to understand in general how sibling loss affects marriage and families, it is necessary to look at why humans grieve at all.

Psychologist John Bowlby believed that humans have a biological tendency to seek connection with significant others whenever threatening circumstances exist. Like children who run to their mothers for safety, adults reach out to others when frightened and tend to move together to face a common threat. When we do this, the bond between us grows stronger. This same process occurs when people are bereaved and grieve together. As we open up to others by grieving with them, love can flow between us, love that begins to heal the broken heart, at the same time that it strengthens the bond between those who are grieving.

Some of us are afraid to feel our painful feelings and put up psychological defense mechanisms to keep the pain away. Unfortunately, this also prevents warm, loving feelings from flowing in to heal the hurt. It gradually creates more and more distance between us until the connection weakens to the point that it is practically non-existent. Some survivors may reach for drugs or alcohol to soothe their pain. Other emotionally starved individuals may begin to seek sexual connections outside of the marriage to feed their hungry hearts. If we want to be happily married, it is crucial to learn to share our pain as well as our joy.

The marriage relationship is not the only place where secondary loss occurs. When an adult sibling dies, his or her spouse and children sometimes move away, and we rarely see them again. So we have lost not only the sibling but also the sibling's family. This has a huge impact on cousins, grandparents, aunts, uncles, nieces, and nephews, as well as siblings and parents.

Cause of the sibling's death also impacts the family afterwards. If the sibling committed suicide, survivors may blame his or her spouse, creating another rift. Anger is a natural reaction to loss and survivors look for someone to blame—the person who seemingly caused the accident, those who failed to visit the dying sibling, the one who didn't do enough to help. Relationships become shaky when family members use each other as targets for their anger.

Family members can support each other and grow strong, or avoid their grief, and become isolated from each other. The family can break into a thousand pieces—putting it back together again may take a long time.

Dealing with Negative Emotions

Adults, because they are emotionally mature, may feel crushed by a conflicting mixture of emotions after the death of a sibling. These are sometimes hard to separate, and last a long time.

Anger

Anger, whether it is acknowledged or not, may be a constant companion after the death. Bereaved adults may not like their new role, having people looking to them to take care of everything. They may not wish to be the only one left to care for aging parents. They may be furious that their sibling died so young. Anger is just one of the many negative emotions that arise from such a profound loss.

Some survivors are surprised at the mixed feelings they experience towards their deceased brother or sister when the death occurs at a significant time in their own lives, such as right before they are getting married, or just after the birth of their child. If they left home recently, such as a young adult just out of college, parents may want them to move back home. Surviving adult siblings may feel that they have to sacrifice their life's plans and ambitions in order to comfort or stay near their parents, and end up angry with the one who died.

Guilt and Remorse

Guilt is another unwelcome emotion after the death of a brother or sister. Sibling relationships are ambivalent by nature. This means that we both love and hate our siblings. Having lived with them for many years, we have fought and argued. Thus there are many reasons for which to berate ourselves when they die. We see them in memory as good, and ourselves as bad.

Guilt is a feeling that builds with time. We feel responsible for violating some unwritten rule of society, or failing to meet our own standards of behavior. That is the surface—underneath this lies the fact that we, as humans, do not like to feel powerless or helpless. We could not prevent our sibling's death—we were utterly powerless. Guilt makes us feel stronger. So we pretend to ourselves that if we had been there, or if we had taken some particular action, things would have been different. Then we blame ourselves for having failed the deceased sibling.

As time passes, we examine our memories of the relationship with the deceased sibling. We find that we have failed before, not been as kind or generous as we should have; we have not lived up to our own code of behavior. So we end up feeling even more guilt.

Some of us may have been embarrassed by our brothers or sisters, or ashamed of them for some reason. Upon their death, this feeling may turn to guilt as we struggle with the belief that we should have tried harder to help them get their lives together. Now, instead of being embarrassed by them, we are ashamed of ourselves, and the memory of how we treated our sibling—even thoughts we had about them—come back in the form of painful remorse.

Increasing self-acceptance can help us live through this kind of guilt. Perhaps we are not as perfect as we thought—perhaps we were too jealous, or too competitive, or downright mean to our sibling when he or she was living. So we are flawed, like everyone else. Welcome to the human race! Working on accepting ourselves, as individuals who do make mistakes, supports us in the grief process.

Sometimes bereaved siblings punish themselves simply for living when their brother or sister is dead—this is survivor guilt. It almost feels like a betrayal of the sibling, for us to go on living. As a clinician, I believe survivor guilt to be a factor in most cases of complicated grief.

Guilt about the death itself stems from the dislike of feeling helpless. Perhaps there was something we could have done to prevent our sibling's death. We should have called him on the phone so that he wouldn't have been in his car and been hit at that exact time. We shouldn't have recommended the restaurant that he was headed towards when he was hit. We should have reminded her to get a yearly medical checkup. It goes on and on. Once we accept that we were, in fact, absolutely helpless, we will feel the pain of the loss at a deeper level.

I hope that, as you read this, you don't think that I am trying to talk you out of your guilt. Not at all. Recovery from guilt can be explained with a simple weight scale. When we have 100 pounds of guilt on one side of the scale, then we need 100 pounds of punishment (or atonement) on the other to balance the scale. Only when we have done so can we forgive ourselves, and enter fully into living. In order to get that 100 pounds of punishment, we have to feel the guilt—not avoid it.

Experienced grievers suggest a number of ways to help with guilt. These include:

- Exercise and feel your guilt while exercising. If you don't usually exercise, take a guilt walk.

- Share every part of your guilt with a trusted friend (someone who has lost a sibling) or therapist.

- Do a good deed for someone or donate money and NEVER TELL ANYONE—Keep it secret.

- Turn your pain into art by writing about it, painting it, or building something you dedicate to the deceased sibling.

- Forgive others and ask forgiveness from God for yourself.

- Consciously atone for whatever sin you feel you have committed by doing some related volunteer work.

Fear and anxiety

Bereaved adults often ask the question: "Am I next?" A sibling's death leads naturally to this thought. Our siblings are our peers so it makes sense that we think in this way. Facing death teaches us forcibly that life has an end, and we, too, are mortal.

We typically believe that older people die first, so when a sibling dies as a young adult, we fear the repetition of what happened, for us or for our children. If we still have children at home, we are likely to become over-protective in an attempt to control fate. Anxiety about the cause of death is inevitable. Individuals whose sibling died in a car accident are likely to have more issues with driving, and be more fearful when their children begin to drive. Those whose sibling died of cancer will more likely visit the doctor sooner when they discover a lump or discolored skin.

The related feelings of confusion and shock arise when the death reveals previously unknown facts about the sibling's life. Some survivors learn that their brother or sister died as a result of alcoholism, drug use, or AIDS. Some learn for the first time that their sibling was gay, or that they had been in jail, had a family no one knew about, or were wanted by the police. Survivors grieve for the part of their sibling they never got to know.

The Little Miracle

There comes a day after a period of mourning, when we wake up and notice that the sky is blue and the sun is shining. We feel as though we have been gone for a long time, but now we are back, and we want to live, in spite of our losses. This gives us the hope we need to go on without our brothers and sisters.

The shattering of the trust we once held in life and the universe cannot be rebuilt overnight. Time alone cannot rebuild this trust. As we tell the story of loss to caring others, however, the fabric of life can be re-woven, our life story also containing the story of our beloved sibling.

The Nest of the Loneliness Birds

In some parts of the world, such as the high mountain plains of South America, and parts of desert Africa, "nests" of stones are found. How is it possible that such smooth, round stones, which are normally found in rivers at much lower elevations, could be high on a mountain or in a desert, where there are no rivers? A primitive myth explains the phenomenon.

The myth says that these are the nests of the loneliness birds. These birds live at high altitudes and are usually seen in silhouette, as they scan the earth, searching for a place to lay their eggs. The stones, lying together in a sandy soil, look so much like smooth eggs. We might be tempted to pick one up, and when we do, we find they are heavy—just like the heaviness we feel in our hearts when we are grieving.

When a loved one dies, so the story goes, the loneliness birds lay their stone eggs in our hearts. We can feel them there, weighing us down, and we live with them for a long time. We become used to carrying this burden within us, and gradually, we grow strong.

One morning, we wake up, and something has changed. The sun is overhead, shining brightly; the sky welcomes us to the world outside. We look around and seem to see our surroundings with new eyes, as if we have been gone for a long time. Even the most mundane objects around us seem to be full of meaning. And we feel light on our feet. During the night, the loneliness birds took their eggs and flew away.

4

Five Healing Tasks

o o o o o o o o o o o o o o o o o o o o o o o o o o o o o o o o
"The only cure for grief is grieving."

—*Folk Wisdom*

One definition of the word "healing" is 'to be restored to wholeness'. When someone we love dies, it feels like a big piece of our heart has been ripped away. Mourners describe feeling shattered, broken up, like everything is coming apart. To heal, or to become whole, after the death of a brother or sister, we have to grow that part inside us with the help of the grief process. We won't be exactly the same as before, but we will be restored to wholeness.

Bereaved siblings themselves describe five tasks that facilitate healing after the death of a brother or sister. These differ markedly from the stages of grief or tasks for grieving that we usually read about, and are specific to sibling loss. The tasks are not to be completed one after another, but are inter-related. They are:

1. **Learning about sibling loss and the grief process**

2. **Allowing yourself to grieve**

3. **Connecting with other bereaved siblings**

4. **Telling your story**

5. **Finding meaning in the loss**

Task 1—Learning about sibling loss and the grief process

Educating ourselves about sibling loss helps provide a way of thinking about it so we can make sense of our feelings. Many people must have this cognitive framework in place before they can trust themselves to feel the pain of loss. Learning about the grief process gives us a vocabulary and a structure through which we can define our experience. This means learning about the phases of grief, whether or not we agree that they are accurate. They give us realistic expectations about the process, and remove some of the fear.

As we consider the phases and stages of grief, we don't have to agree with any particular theory. In fact, we could each make up our own theory of grief stages, based on our own experience. Who else is better qualified? Learning about the stages, however, helps us to put our experience into a specific context. This feels better than living with the vague ill-defined "soup" of mixed emotions and thoughts about the loss.

At one time, experts talked about a mostly emotional grief process: shock, denial, anger, and sadness that ended with "letting go of the deceased". Another popular theory of grief stages came mistakenly from Elisabeth Kubler-Ross's stages of dying (which described the stages one goes through upon learning of one's own impending death)—denial, anger, bargaining, depression, and acceptance. The most recent views of the grief process, however, describe both an emotional response and a response in our thought processes, followed by an adjustment to the change, but with a continued connection to the one who died.

De-fusing myths

Society encourages myths about grief and loss that prevent us from grieving. The belief that siblings don't suffer much from the death of a brother or sister, the idea that only weak people cry or grieve, the idea that we shouldn't make people feel bad by sharing our grief—all of these distorted notions about grief fail to support us when we need it most.

Our grief must be validated, both by us and preferably by the important people in our lives. This is where sibling loss so often differs from other kinds of loss. Society in general does not acknowledge the pain of losing a sibling, and has unrealistic ideas about how long sibling grief lasts. Sometimes people come to my office and say something like "My sister (or brother) died three months ago and I still feel bad—what is wrong with me? Shouldn't I be over this by now?" They are still learning about the strength of the sibling bond. Their questions reflect those of society in general.

People may not recognize the close ties between siblings, ties that create so much emotional turmoil when death tears them apart. Validation of our feelings is the first step in allowing ourselves to express those feelings so that we can heal. It allows us to tell the story of the loss.

To dispel the myth that sibling loss is not significant, bereaved siblings need to trust their own feelings. Even if no one around us believes we have the right to grieve, we know in our hearts that our feelings make sense. Our sibling was part of our early lives, our formative lives, and part of who we are. Siblings know us like no one else can. Of course, it is painful! Although we may not have had a close adult relationship with a sibling, we still feel that we have lost our play-mates, part of our shared childhoods. No wonder we are grieving!

Comparing and contrasting

Learning about the impact of sibling loss on others in similar circumstances is another way to help us think about what happened. Every time we read about someone else's experience or watch a movie about sibling loss, we have an oppor-tunity to sort out our experience. We can say to ourselves, "my experience wasn't like that" or "that's exactly what I felt." This process of turning the experience over in our minds offers several benefits:

- Comparing and contrasting our experiences helps us to work it through. This works somewhat like a rock tumbler—we put in jagged rocks and tumble them until they become smooth. As we think and feel about what happened, some of the painful emotion is drained away, leaving the mem-ory, but without the emotional charge.

- It helps us tell our story. We may not know how to talk about what hap-pened to us, but when we read another person's story, we can describe our experiences by comparison.

- It helps us define and shape our experiences. It allows us to look at our experiences through a new set of eyes, as if we are seeing it from outside. This helps us to be compassionate towards ourselves.

Task 2—Allowing Yourself to Grieve

There have been many attempts to describe the grief process, but all of them include the fact that we must first become aware of the reality of the loss and then feel the subsequent pain.

Accepting the reality of the loss is not the same as agreeing with the fact that it happened. Most people do accept the reality that death occurred, once the initial shock wears off. (Only in rare cases do individuals pretend that their sibling is still alive.) However, most of us try to avoid feeling pain whenever we can. Some people turn to drugs and alcohol to numb pain, while others use frantic activity, working long hours, or rushing mindlessly from one activity to another, to avoid it.

To recognize and accept that we are experiencing grief sounds simple, but for those individuals who have spent a lifetime keeping their feelings locked away, it may not be so easy. As soon as feelings surface, a barrage of self-condemnation and self-criticism begins:

"You have to be strong!"

"You can't show your weakness."

"Crying is for sissies!"

"Don't break down!"

We internalize these messages based on what we have learned from the important people in our lives. We are born with the capacity to feel and experience a wide range of emotion. When we don't express them, it may be because we fear our feelings will be judged, or that we don't want to expose our weakness. Our cultural values encourage us to judge certain feelings as bad or wrong, which makes us hide unacceptable feelings. This prevents us from bringing all our emotions into our relationships, so they can by shared and mature. When we DO feel one of these unacceptable feelings, it is still immature and makes us feel babyish, as if we are still three years old.

The word emotion comes from two words that mean, "to move out". These two parts of the word teach us about emotion. First, that it is moving. We won't get "stuck" in our feelings if we express them—they move through us. Second, that they are meant to move out of us, by being felt. What keeps them stuck is NOT feeling and expressing them. When we express our feelings, they help us understand the world. They warn us of danger, tell us when our needs are being met, when we are being mistreated, or that we have lost something we need.

Grief is a natural part of life. People won't break into pieces because they are grieving. The way to get beyond the grief is to feel it. Some people mistakenly believe that not thinking about the loss and not expressing their grief will make it go away in time. The statement: "What you RESIST, PERSISTS" is true. This means that when we resist the feelings, they will persist, much like a nagging child who stands beside us tugging at our clothes to get our attention.

Sad feelings must be felt in order to subside. We suffer far more pain from trying not to cry, for example, than we do when actually crying. There are toxins in emotional tears and crying releases them. So we really do feel better.

With courage, we can learn to be pro-active with our grief. We don't have to passively allow grief to eat away our lives. We can use this energy in creative pursuits, writing, drawing, painting, and music—effectively turning our pain into art of some kind. We can pro-actively access our memories on our own schedules, looking through photo albums and allowing the memories to surface. We can spend the energy participating in some activity that our sibling would have enjoyed.

Task 3—Connecting with other bereaved siblings

One outcome of sibling loss that is mentioned again and again in research is the fact that bereaved siblings feel different from their peers. We need to feel that we belong; it is one of our most basic needs. Meeting other bereaved siblings reduces this sense of isolation, especially for those who have no support at home. No one understands as well as those who have been through it. A sense of connection often develops quickly between bereaved siblings.

At the moment we learn that our brother or sister is going to die or has died, some of us begin to form a special place within us to contain this experience and keep it away from the rest of our lives. This protected space keeps others away from our pain and our experience. Other bereaved siblings can often get inside this space when no one else can. Once we open this part of ourselves to another person whom we trust, healing can begin.

We can find other bereaved siblings in support groups, and some of these are listed in chapter 9. Many websites offer online support in the form of message boards and listservs. When we become more open about our experiences, other bereaved siblings will approach us with their stories. If it is not possible to meet others in person, it can also help to meet them in literature, either in fiction or memoirs

Task 4—Telling your story

In order to heal, we must integrate our sibling's death experience into our own life story, and then know that our stories do go on. Our stories do not end at the death of our siblings. But it is in the telling of the story to another person that we feel the loss most deeply and learn in detail what it is we have lost. Putting our feelings into words links together the emotion with the experience, and keeps us connected to the world of the living.

Grieving alone, by ourselves, may prolong our grief. When we put our feelings into words and express them to another human being, we have the best chance of a complete recovery, provided the other person is a caring individual who will not judge us. If someone says, "You shouldn't feel that way," or "Well, let me tell you what happened to me!" that is the signal to stop sharing with him or her until you have explained what you need.

It is important to allow others to help us at this time. If necessary, we can teach people how to listen. We can tell them we need for them to just sit with us and hear what we have to say, that we simply need them to be with us. Our hearts will tell us who is safe. People who have once experienced and survived grief themselves are often the best source of support.

Another part of healing is in owning our own pain. If we project our painful feelings onto others and attempt to take care of those others, it will not help us. This is such a human response. A bereaved young woman, Nancy, tells her boy-friend, Roger, about the death of her sister, and Roger responds by saying, "Oh, I'm so sorry!" Immediately, *Nancy tries to comfort Roger*, reaching out to touch his arm, saying, "No, no, it's OK, I'm OK".

Actually, it's not OK! Her sister just died—it is not OK. But she doesn't want to make Roger feel bad. This illustrates the difficulty humans have with the expression of painful emotions. We tend to believe that the other person feels terrible when we have expressed our sorrow to them. This is simply not true. Feelings connect people, like a river that flows between them. Usually, expressing grief with supportive loved ones makes people feel closer.

In the most recent theories about what happens in the grief process, experts believe that telling our stories is an important vehicle for integrating the loss. We must create a new life story, one that both includes the death of the beloved sibling, and also progresses from that point on. To do that, we need to find ways of telling the story of the loss and all that happened surrounding it.

Writing the story can also be helpful, particularly if we then read aloud what we have written to someone who can listen and sit with us patiently while we cry. There is a powerful force for healing in the actual voicing of what we have written. We may have to read the story aloud many times to become familiar with it and begin to experience the loss as part of our complete life stories, rather than the end of it.

Task 5—Finding meaning in the loss

What is this thing "meaning" that seems to be noticed only by its absence? One way to understand it is to imagine a tree that has been struck by lightning and become separated from its roots. It may still be standing, but it has been cut off from what it needs to sustain it. Just a slight wind can blow it over. Meaning makes us feel connected at a deep level. As humans, we are like the aspen trees that look like any other tree from above ground, but underneath, have roots that connect them to each other. When we have a sense of meaning in our lives we feel connected not only to ourselves, but also to everyone else. We know that we are not alone.

Meaning includes emotional, physical, relational, and spiritual components. A separation at the root level from any of these components robs life of joy and contentment.

After the death of a sibling, we may become separated from our emotional roots by pushing the grief aside, and not expressing our feelings as they surface.

Anger, in particular, is a separating emotion that blocks out love and tender feelings. Once we have lived in that state for a long time, it doesn't take a tornado to blow us over—even a small thing, like criticism, a minor frustration, or the kids walking on the kitchen floor with muddy feet, can set us into a rage. That is the accumulated anger coming out. We've held it down for so long that it has become monstrous, and almost seems to possess us like alien beings.

Some of us go into our minds as a way to avoid feelings—which are located more in the body—and thus become separated from our earthly roots. Eventually, we may feel that life is unreal, that we are simply floating, and have no connection to other people. The feeling of "panic" often terrifies us, when we have not felt our feelings for many years. We need to become accustomed to having a heartbeat, to moving our bodies. Sports, dance, or even simply walking can help us by getting us in touch with our five senses, and back to a sense of living on the earth.

Bereaved siblings in particular may have lost touch with their relational roots. We are sometimes conflicted about the very relationships with other people that bring meaning to life. We both want and fear the same thing—connection. We need to come to grips with this conflict consciously before it destroys good relationships. Our fear of losing a relationship may actually make us behave in ways that will bring about the loss of a significant other. We may try to control the other so they won't leave us, but our controlling manner drives the person away. We may not allow ourselves to have fun for fear of losing control, so our children or partner find other, more engaging, companions. Becoming aware of these behaviors is the first step towards change.

A lack of meaning might also indicate that we have become separated from our spiritual roots. We are fed spiritually by feeling that we are part of something bigger than us. That might be a higher power, a sense of transcendent beauty, or a deep connection to family. Some people find that going to their house of worship helps to re-connect them with their spiritual roots. Others choose to re-connect through solitude in nature or listening to music.

We find meaning when we change our values or priorities as a result of an experience. For some it takes the form of greater appreciation of life. "I celebrate life now," writes Angie. "I treasure each moment and notice little things—a sunset, the sound of children's voices when they are playing, the color of leaves. I want to honor my brother by living life to the fullest. He had just begun to unwrap the gift of life. I feel that I can make up for what he missed by cherishing it all—the good and the bad."

Others say that they have learned the value of relationships. "I never go to bed angry now," says Louise, "I always say 'I love you'. I learned the hard way that it may be the last time. I think to myself, I need to communicate this now, whatever my feelings may be, and not wait. Relationships are precious."

Some change their behavior based on the way their sibling died. "Every time I buckle my seatbelt," says Scott, "I think about Dave. If I would forget to buckle up, his death would have been in vain. I teach my kids about it too." Writes Marisa, "I go to the doctor for a checkup every year, faithfully. She waited too long and it killed her. When the time comes every year for a mammogram or Pap smear, I can almost hear her saying—go on Marisa, make the appointment. In so many ways, I don't take my health or life for granted any more."

Another way that people find meaning is in helping others who are going through the same experience. "I became a grief counselor," says James, "because it was the only way to make sense of the whole thing. I know that I have used what happened to help people. I had to get degrees and licenses, but they wouldn't have meant anything without the experience itself."

Summary

The five tasks described by hundreds of bereaved siblings show us a pathway to healing. It means learning about sibling loss and the grief process, allowing ourselves to grieve, connecting with other bereaved siblings, telling our stories, and finally, finding meaning in the loss. To be fully human means to embrace the whole experience of life, the highs and lows of emotion, the sensory joys and pains, the risk of relationship, and the connection with a transcendent power. This is where meaning lies. If we are open to it, life itself will guide us to the people and information we need most.

The Legend of the Tear Jar

In the dry climate of ancient Greece, water was prized above all else. Giving up water from one's own body, when crying tears for the dead, was considered a sacrifice. They caught each other's precious tears in tiny pitchers, bottles, or tear jars like the life-sized one shown here. These tears became holy water and could be sprinkled on doorways to keep out evil, or to cool the brow of a sick child.

The tear jars were kept plain and unpainted until the owner experienced the death of a parent, sibling, child, or spouse. After that, the grieving person decorated the tear jar with intricate designs, and examples of these can still be seen throughout modern Greece.

This ancient custom symbolizes the transformation that takes place in people who have grieved deeply. They have not so much "gotten over" their grief, but "grown through" it. They appreciate relationships more. They appreciate life more. They find meaning in little things.

Those whom grief has transformed are not threatened by the grief of other people in pain. They have been in the depths of pain themselves, and returned. Like the tear jar, they can now sit with those who mourn and catch their tears.

5

Thoughts, Actions, Feelings of Grief

o o o o o o o o o o o o o o o o o o o o o o o o o o o o o o o o o o o

Anger as soon as fed is dead—
'Tis starving that makes it fat.

—*Emily Dickinson*

In this chapter, we'll see some of the ways that the thinking, behavior (actions), and emotions (feelings) change after the death of a brother or sister. Grief affects not only our emotions, but also the way we think and our actions.

Thinking

One of the symptoms of trauma for all ages is a tendency to regress to an "either/ or" or black-and-white way of thinking. This happens because one of our basic instincts is to fight or flee when something threatening occurs. When survival is concerned, we don't have time to see the shades of gray, but must act swiftly, based on an either/or decision. This polarized, "all or nothing" thinking makes us see the world or specific people as all good or all bad.

After a death, this kind of thinking may make us more judgmental, even though before the death, we considered ourselves tolerant. When people say things like "Are you all better now?" a week after the funeral, we may consider their question ridiculous, and label them "all bad", but with time are able to see that they are not all bad, just ignorant of what grief is like. We may make sweeping assumptions about life, and say things like "I will always feel this bad," or "Things will never get back to normal." With time and healing, however, we realize that we do feel better and there is a new 'normal'.

While this way of thinking in absolutes may be helpful in terms of survival, it does not help when we have to carry on with life while feeling torn apart inside. Decision-making may be extremely difficult for a while. The ability to concentrate becomes impaired. We may have memory lapses about what happened and think we are going crazy.

Actions

Grief is much like a physical illness. The actions associated with grief are called mourning. Mourners feel weak and can scarcely get out of bed. They wring their hands and pace back and forth. They sigh over and over because they can't seem to catch their breath. They cry and cannot sleep. They sleep too much. They can't eat and lose thirty pounds, or they eat too much and gain thirty pounds. They have no energy—they get headaches or stomachaches, dizziness, and panic attacks.

When mourners do get up and move around, their activity is purposeless. They walk into the kitchen, but can't remember why; they wander listlessly through the house. They tremble and their heart beats rapidly. They feel like they are getting physically ill. They typically withdraw and want to stay around the house because they feel exhausted and weak. On the other hand, some mourners become so active that they rush around, cleaning house or busying themselves at some task, any task. They have to be moving constantly, so they won't think and won't feel.

Some behaviors of mourning are attachment behaviors. The purpose of these actions, such as crying, calling, and protesting are to get the lost person back. We believe these instinctive actions have survival value, in that they help a child maintain closeness to the parent, much like a lamb bleating to find its mother.

The mourning behavior of children and teens may be "acting out", where they are acting out a feeling that they cannot put into words. In this case, they are seeking attention from the parent in order to feel safe. They feel insecure so they behave in ways that get the parent to be "parental", which reminds them that they are still just kids, and Mom and Dad are in charge.

Feelings

The feelings associated with grief are many and may go on for a long time. Whether a sibling died recently or long ago, we may find that we still have significant emotional energy around specific issues.

The basic families of emotions are sometimes called Mad, Sad, Bad, and Glad.

The "Mad" Family of Feelings

The Mad Family includes all the emotions related to anger, such as Angry, Bitter, Ripped off, Contemptuous, Outraged, Annoyed, Furious, Used, Resentful, Frustrated, Insulted, Irritated, Offended, Cynical, Defensive, Vengeful, Sarcastic, On fire, Burned, Abusive, Destructive, Mean, Antagonistic, Indignant, Fed-up, Sullen, Disdainful, Enraged.

The feelings in this family are secondary feelings, those that surface after the primary feeling of fear or hurt. A person who is angry, in other words, is a person who is hurt or afraid. Anger usually makes us feel stronger. Anger that is not expressed and worked through can go on for a long time indeed.

Why are survivor siblings still mad—days, months, or even years after the death of their brother or sister? Here are some of the reasons:

- Parents or other relatives, or friends did not acknowledge the loss of their brother or sister.
- The disturbing manner in which they got the news of the death
- Having to be the one who told everyone else of the death.
- Others expected them to take care of the parents.
- How they were treated immediately after hearing the news.
- Some were ignored, some were sent to stay with a relative.
- Some were not given any information.
- Because of the way that they, or another sibling, was treated in the months and years after the loss. For example, some were blamed for not being the one who died; some were targeted as a scapegoat for the parent's anger.

- Their peers had no awareness of the reality of life and death, so they felt as if they were now different from them.

- Because life went on as normal.

- They were not allowed to grieve

- No one talked about the death and the dead sibling was never mentioned.

- The sibling's spouse doesn't seem upset.

- Anger at people who say "I know how you feel," "All better now?" and other insensitive comments.

- They don't agree with some aspect of the funeral, burial site, or gravestone—issues like not having a gravestone, the wording on the gravestone.

- They don't feel the sibling got the appropriate care while in hospital.

- Not knowing what happened to the sibling or the body during the last minutes or hours prior to or after the death.

- They saw the body in a broken and wounded state, after a car accident, for example.

- They were not allowed or encouraged to go to or participate in the funeral.

- They did not get to see the body.

- They didn't know how to deal with their feelings.

- They weren't informed about the severity of their sibling's illness.

- Someone else survived who was involved in the accident that killed his or her sibling.

- They had to baby-sit, clean house, or be responsible for other chores while parents were at the hospital, sheriff's office, funeral home…

- No one ever asked how they were feeling. They often heard "How are your parents?"

- That someone erased a telephone voice message from the deceased sibling.

- That they had to grow up overnight.

- They were blamed for acting out and trying to get attention, when they were too young to understand what was really happening.

- They were over-protected after the loss.

- They were expected to "become" the dead sibling or make up for their loss, or they were the only one left to produce grandchildren.

- They didn't get a chance to say good-bye.

- Frustration arising from problems associated with language difficulties, such as doctors who don't speak English.

- Co-workers who expected them to be perfectly normal when they got back to work.

- Other people pretending that everything is normal or not even mentioning the loss.

- The dead sibling's belongings were given away or disposed of without their knowledge or consent.

- They can't see their dead sibling's children

- Not knowing the actual cause of death.

- That their brother or sister committed suicide or was murdered.

- That the murderer gets to live.

- Getting "fake" support, as when someone asks how they are just to get attention and then rushes the subject on to something else.

Anger is energy. Professional athletes draw on their anger energy at times when they need courage or endurance. People sometimes use their anger to bring about change. These are positive uses of anger. If anger is a problem for us, we may need professional help to bring the primary feelings to the surface so we can work them through.

The "SAD" Family of Feelings

The feelings in this family are those we most often associate with the loss of any loved one. The death of a sibling leaves an emotional bruise, which can easily bring back sad feelings each time it is touched in future years.

The Sad family of feelings includes: Despondent, Grief-stricken, Sorrowing, Martyred, Regretful, Remorseful, Hurt, Empty, Undeserving, Useless, Hopeless, Pathetic, Pitiful, Alone, Upset, Lonely, Unwanted, Rejected, Unloved, Alienated, Depressed, Sorry, Down In the dumps, Worthless, Insignificant, Tearful, Self-defeating, Regret, Needy, Disillusioned, Forgotten, Left out, Suicidal, Wounded, Broken hearted, Blue, Inadequate, Discounted, and Abandoned.

Bereaved siblings still feel sorrow and sadness from the many losses associated with the death of a brother or sister.

- The loss of companionship and a future with their sibling.

- Loss of a playmate, confidant, or best friend.

- Loss, at least for a time, of the parents while they were grieving.

- Loss of parts of the self that were projected onto the deceased sibling.

- Loss of innocence.

- Missing out on peer related activities.

- Feeling left out.

- Sadness at witnessing the dead sibling's children growing up without a parent.

- Not getting the attention they needed to deal with such a profound loss.

- Being lonely.

- That there is now a hole when they visit their other siblings, because it is then obvious that one is missing. The presence of other family members reminds them forcibly of this fact.

- Sorry that they can't go back and make up for something they did or said.

- Their sibling's spouse moved away so they can't see their nieces and nephews any more.

- Loss of support when they are the only ones left to take care of their parents.

- Loss of trust in people and life in general

- Loss of trust in doctors, or the legal system

- Sadness about having to move house after the death.

- Sadness about subsequent, associated losses, such as divorce.

It is an unfortunate fact that many individuals who experienced an early loss suffer from a kind of permanent sadness, called "dysthymia", which is defined as a low-grade, long-term depression. It is as if a cloud of gloom surrounds them. Dysthymia can be treated with medication and psychotherapy. Remember that grief comes and goes, but dysthymia is more of a permanent feeling of sadness.

The "Bad" Family of Feelings

This family of feelings includes feelings associated with fear and guilt such as: Ashamed, Embarrassed, Fearful, Threatened, Frightened, Anxious, Dismayed, Apprehensive, Disturbed, Torn, Conflicted, Miserable, Panicky, Humiliated, Shocked, Trapped, Horrified, Afraid, Scared, Terrified, Edgy, Nervous, Tense, Worried, Perplexed, Bewildered, Mixed-up, Uncomfortable, Troubled, Alarmed, Confused, Fed-up, Baffled, Dissatisfied, Shaky, Upset, Guilty, Culpable, Responsible, and Blamed.

In the years following the death of a brother or sister, siblings often have significant difficulty with fear and guilt.

- Fear of doctors and hospitals.
- Fear of doing whatever the sibling was doing that led to the death—such as swimming, driving, or horseback riding.
- Fear of their own children's death.
- Watchfulness for symptoms related to the sibling's illness
- Having the sense that they will not live long.
- Fear that something else bad will happen.
- Anxiety about their parents' deaths.
- Guilt about fights with the deceased sibling.
- Guilt about how they acted at the time of the illness, for example, going out with friends instead of staying with their siblings.
- Guilt about possibly causing the death, for example by giving their sibling a disease.
- Guilt about going on with life, surviving at all, or for being happy.
- Guilt about a number of things they did or didn't do prior to the death.
- Fear that they will forget their sibling
- Fear of change, wanting everything to stay the same, fear of leaving the town where the sibling is buried
- Fear that they are going crazy or are "cracking up" or that they are not like other people
- Fear of being the same age as the age of the sibling who died.

- Fear of their children being the same age as the age of the sibling who died.

- Guilt about being the sole remaining child and inheriting everything from parents when they die; especially for those who jokingly fought about "who got what" when the sibling was alive.

The "Glad" Family of Feelings

The feelings in this family are typically those we wish we had all the time. We might think, "How could any of these emotions relate to someone who lost a sibling?" In the midst of grief, we can still feel loved by those who support us, comforted by the relatives who come in to the funeral, and gratified that they did make the trip.

This family includes: Calm, Relaxed, Peaceful, Happy, Connected, Inspired, Amused, Pleased, Relieved, Ecstatic, Joyous, Serene, Loved, Encouraged, Excited, Affectionate, Appreciated, Enthusiastic, Patient, Esteemed, Liked, Courageous, Zealous, Cared for, Hopeful, Optimistic, Eager, Proud, Jolly, Friendly, Gratified, Delighted, Sure, Alert, Comforted, Accepted, Content, Helpful, Respected, Consoled, Included, Tender, Capable, Adored, Untroubled, Nurtured, Worthy, Vibrant, Gratified, and Welcoming.

Bereaved siblings, who look back on their experience, describe feeling glad about a number of issues. Not every bereaved sibling has the same experience, but here are some of the reasons…

- They feel loved and supported by friends and family

- They appreciate life and relationships.

- They have a deeper spiritual life.

- They still feel connected to the deceased sibling.

- Life is more real to them.

- Some say they no longer fear death.

- They have the sense of being guarded by an angel.

- When troubled in other relationships, they feel that their deceased sibling is always on their side.

- When they engage in activities once shared with their sibling, they feel the presence of that sibling.

- The kindness of others who support them by listening, sending cards or gifts like stuffed animals, hugs, and offering practical assistance, such as picking up children at school or doing grocery shopping.

- Realizing that some of the qualities and characteristics of the deceased sibling are shared by others in the family and even friends.

- That they can still participate in activities their sibling enjoyed.

- Glad that they have faith in an afterlife where they will one day see their sibling again.

- Glad that they are not alone and have other siblings to share their grief.

Our thinking and our actions will most likely return to normal in a short time after a loss. Feelings, however, can go on for a lifetime.

Sorrow

She rises out of nowhere, like a wave from the sea,
Slowly at first, silently, then crests and peaks;
Still I have a choice
I can turn away, go to work, watch a movie, play a game...

But I know sorrow well.
Though I turn away, she will wait,
perfectly patient,
until I am still,
then crush me with all of her accumulated power.

Once I had angry walls to shut her out,
But her incessant pounding tore them down.
So now, when she rises,
I turn to her and say,
Here I am, I know you, sorrow.
She crashes on my shoreline,
And sorrow and I are one
Until, trailing frothy whitecaps,
She sweeps away.

P.G. White

6

Long-term Effects of Sibling Loss

○ ○

The holiest of all holidays are those
Kept by ourselves in silence and apart,
The secret anniversaries of the heart.

—Bereaved parent, Henry Wadsworth Longfellow

There is a story, undoubtedly apocryphal, about Freud, who was sitting around with his colleagues, discussing the illness that brought most people to see them. "What shall we call that disease that adults have who lost a parent or sibling during childhood?" he asked. His friends put their heads together and replied, "Let's call it Depression."

Bereaved siblings entering therapy for depression may have no idea that this is related to the death of their brother or sister years before. It is often around mid-life when bereaved siblings no longer have the energy to maintain their suppressed and repressed emotions. Perhaps their children have reached the age they were when their sibling died, or the age their sibling was when he or she got sick. Or it may be a loss such as a divorce or being fired from their job that triggers the lifting of repression.

It doesn't seem fair that young people should have to go through this event twice—once when it actually happens, and again when they are finally strong enough to deal with the feelings. But when something so traumatic happens, we hide the event within us, and go about the business of growing up. In many families, the loss is never discussed, and no one seeks treatment, so there is no way to process the event.

This is a puzzling characteristic of our society. We know about the importance of processing events. Even school children are routinely given the opportunity to process special events (like going to the zoo) by writing or drawing pictures about them. But when a sibling dies, we pretend it didn't happen. We warn our children about the dangers of everything from talking to strangers to tooth decay, but don't help them work through a major loss. It just doesn't make sense. Many of the long-term effects could be avoided if the processing were done at the time of the loss, instead of years later.

I have often been asked what is the most difficult age to lose a sibling or what circumstances make sibling loss more difficult. These questions cannot be answered by anyone but the mourner. As a clinician, however, I can make some observations about a sibling's death, which follows a many-years-long illness. These survivors cannot look back and pick out that one single event that changed their life forever. There are so many events over such a long period that they blur into one large stain that seeps through all of their young lives. On the one hand, they had more time to say good-bye and get used to the idea that their sibling was too sick to go on living. On the other hand, however, they had more time to do and say things they might later regret.

Anniversary reactions

One of the most troublesome long-term reactions to sibling loss is called an "anniversary reaction," when grief returns in full force on or near

- The anniversary of the sibling's death
- His or her birthday
- Holiday times
- While listening to certain music
- Transitional events, such as a re-location, promotion, marriage...

Our subconscious mind is a ruthless timekeeper where loss is concerned. It is as if we have a calendar within us. Often without even being consciously aware of the date, acute pain surfaces, and we begin to feel terrible, but we don't associate the emotional pain with the loss that happened long ago. At other times, even though we are aware of the reason for the pain, it is still intense, and feels as if it will last forever.

What helps survivors deal with anniversary reactions? Sometimes, simply becoming aware of the date can help reduce the pain. Since anniversary reactions may come up decades later, this is more difficult than you might imagine.

Jonathan: "When my brother died, I had no idea that it would continue to have an effect on my life, even now when I am 15 years older than I was then. My brother, Brian, died on April 19th, and last year, as that date approached, I began to feel terrible. But I didn't realize that it had anything to do with Brian's death. It seemed like everyone in the family was against me.

My kids were annoying me deliberately. My wife got on my nerves constantly and I was thinking that everything was her fault. One day I answered the phone, and happened to look at the calendar next to the phone. Suddenly, it hit me. April 19th! A surge of grief came over me, and I had to hand the phone to my wife.

I went into the bedroom and started to cry. It seemed like yesterday—he was sixteen years old and I was seventeen. He was in a car wreck. A truck plowed into him as he turned into the bowling alley. He went into a coma, and they thought he was coming around, but suddenly, his brain swelled up and he died.

This year, I was prepared. I gave the flowers at church in my brother's memory. It was easier to get through the end of April this year."

Differences for children

Children also experience such phenomena, but not in exactly the same way as adults. While adults are more likely to be aware of the date on which their sibling died, children may not remember the exact date. Instead, they think in terms of events that have specific meaning for them.

They talk about missing their brother or sister mostly on holidays and birthdays. They also recall their sibling during certain weather conditions, for example, when it snows, and they remember going out to play in the snow, or when it is hot and they are going swimming. Any special treat, such as going to a theme park or baseball game, may bring their sibling to mind and cause them to start thinking about the deceased brother or sister and wishing they could share the good times.

Bert: "Mom, Dad, it's snowing! Can we go outside? Boy, I bet Jeff is happy now, watching us from Heaven. Do you think he can still see us through the snow?"

The following list presents a sampling of other triggers for these reactions:

- Becoming the same age your sibling was when he or she died.
- Having your children become that age.
- Having another loss, such as your children leaving home for college.
- Family reunions, when you get together with other siblings and become aware that one is missing.
- Listening to music
- When life is good and you realize that your sibling is missing it all.

Related phenomena

While some experts clump all anniversary reactions together, some differentiate those where the mourner is grieving for the person their sibling would have become.

Marie: Marie's 14-year-old sister, Teresa, committed suicide when Marie was 22 years old. A decade later, when Marie was getting married, she experienced a return of the initial grief. "She won't be here to be my maid of honor," sobs Marie. "It was what we planned when we were little girls. I miss the grown-up Teresa, the friend she would have been now."

Alice: "It never occurred to me that I would be sad about my sister's death when my first child was born. At first, I was so happy. Then I realized that if my sister had lived, she would be so happy for me. It seemed like I was losing not the young girl who died from leukemia when she was eight years old and I was ten, but the grown-up MaryAnn would have become. She would have been my best friend, the aunt to my child; she would have been joyous because of this birth. I was happy and sad at the same time."

Returning memories

The trauma of early sibling loss is so intense that it stamps upon the young person's mind memories that correspond to each and every detail surrounding the loss.

We know from current research over the lifespan that the good things that happen to us in early life (rather than the painful things) are better predictors of how our lives will turn out. When bereaved siblings start talking about what happened, they find both painful and uplifting memories begin to surface.

The memories that returned for me were sometimes dark and ugly, like the woman who attacked my mother when she learned that her son would not get my sister's corneas—the cancer had destroyed them. Other memories shone like jewels. One day I was with my sister in the hospital when we heard a gurney rattling up the hallway. Linda started crying because it meant she had to take the painful, bone-shaking trip down to Radiation. I cried too.

Suddenly, she stopped crying and her smile lit the room as she gasped, "Oh, I'm so glad it's you!"

At the door was a giant of a man, an African-American orderly with an answering smile. Immediately, he was all action and joking, getting us to laugh.

"You must be the sister I've heard so much about!" he said, reaching over with his long arms to pull the bedding loose. With one graceful sweeping movement, he lifted Linda into his arms with the blankets and sheets all around her, like a cocoon. "Now don't worry about her—I'll have her back here in a jiffy! Just wait right here."

Since he was strong enough to carry her down to Radiation, he could keep her from the jolting pain of the gurney ride. I followed them to the door and then peeked out and watched as he stepped into the elevator and turned around. Linda's blonde head leaned trustingly against his shoulder and he looked forward, not realizing that I could see him. His eyes were full of pain and tears. Years later, I saw a photo of the Pieta, Michelangelo's statue of Mary holding the broken body of Jesus, and I recognized the compassion I had seen that day.

The Right Key for the Lock

Years and even decades later, these memories can be activated, and bereaved siblings will experience emotion about something seemingly insignificant. Sometimes the emotion is separated from the event that caused it. At those times, it is important to ask ourselves "How is what is going on here like something that happened to me earlier?"

We are not going crazy. Human behavior does make sense. As we make connections between our responses now and our earlier loss, we begin to understand and feel more comfortable with ourselves. It is as if we have tried several keys in a keyhole and can't find the right one, but suddenly the key clicks into place and opens the door. Kerplunk! Now we understand! The portion of energy that we used to keep the feelings and memory hidden can now be utilized for our day-to-day life.

John: "My oldest brother died in a car accident when he was seventeen and I was ten. When my parents got the call and went to the hospital, we had a red-haired teenaged neighbor come to stay with us.

Decades later, when I was a parent, my wife hired a young girl to stay with our kids when we went to a movie. When the babysitter arrived, I immediately felt a sense of impending doom, almost terror. I was afraid to leave for the movie. I am not the kind of person who experiences psychic phenomena, so I was puzzled by the intensity of my reaction. My wife and I fought about my irrational decision to stay home and I ended up seeing a counselor. I began to wonder what was going on with me. Was I going crazy?

In therapy, as I talked about this, I suddenly realized that this babysitter also had red hair. I cried as the memory came back of the night my parents went to the hospital to find out that Stevie had died there."

As a child, John did not feel that sense of impending doom. Perhaps he was so young that feeling all of his feelings would have overwhelmed him. Perhaps he was in shock. The trigger of a red-haired babysitter activated the feelings, but without the accompanying memory.

My example: One day my husband asked me to hold the door open while he carried our computer out, which he was taking to be repaired. He was trying to be extra careful not to damage this precious piece of equipment. As I held open the door, and he left, I suddenly burst into tears.

We all love our computers but I knew this reaction was way out of line! I sat down and asked myself how this event was like something that happened earlier. Suddenly the memory surfaced of the last night my sister spent at home. She had started hemorrhaging in the middle of the night. My mother told me to stand by the door and hold it for the paramedics. As they carried my sister out on a stretcher, I held the door open and they left. I remember just standing there with the door open for a long time.

There is no easy formula for healing because sometimes you have to wait for the right key to open that door. Because of the complexity of sibling relationships, we can't possibly do all of our grieving at once.

Danny, age 44, felt sad every time his wife talked about going on vacation. His response was so unusual and he felt even more confused about his reaction—feeling sad when you would think he would be happy—that he asked himself this question. "How is what is happening now LIKE what happened around the time when my brother died?"

The answer came to him immediately. His family was on vacation when his older brother, who was in college, was in a traffic accident. Within minutes of returning home, they had received a call informing them that Jerry, his brother, was in the hospital, where he later died. Danny had consciously forgotten about the vacation that preceded Jerry's death, but his subconscious remembered. Once he made the connection, and found a rational explanation for his emotional state, the emotions themselves subsided.

Rules for living

Some of the long-term effects of early loss are associated with "rules for living" created by childlike thinking. Children learn from traumatic and painful events. They create rules of behavior that they believe, with their child-like logic, will prevent the trauma from re-occurring. Many adults are being guided from within by such rules that they created as children. Here are some examples:

Rule: Never trust adults (or something terrible will happen)

Some bereaved siblings feel betrayed by parents and others who led them to believe that only old people die. They tell themselves: never trust grownups! Later, as adults, they may hang on to these beliefs, distrusting authorities, an attitude that may cause them difficulty with teachers and employers.

Rule: Never get sick (or something terrible will happen)

They see doctors as powerless to protect them from sickness and death, so they tell themselves: never get sick! They may become afraid of even minor physical problems and obsess about germs and disease to the point that they do not enjoy life.

Rule: Never get skinny (or something terrible will happen)

In studies on sibling loss due to cancer, several individuals reported that they couldn't allow themselves to get too thin, because of their association between thinness and impending death.

Rule: Never show your anger (or something terrible will happen)

Siblings troubled by guilt about an angry fight with their sibling may decide that anger is far too dangerous an emotion. They try to live their lives suppressing anger, which doesn't work, so they become depressed.

These naïve rules, set during a time of heightened emotional response, wield power over a lifetime. Psychotherapy or counseling can help to discover and neutralize their power.

Vulnerability to loss

Siblings who have lost brothers or sisters remain vulnerable to future losses, so that they may over-react, even to seemingly insignificant losses. They might, in fact, become over-protective of their own children, passing the impact of the loss on to the next generation. If their sibling drowned, they may not allow their children to go swimming. If he or she died in a car accident, they may delay allowing their children to get driver's licenses, and suffer terrible anxiety when their children do start driving. Such vulnerability sometimes results in a pessimistic style of thinking that colors all of life.

Bereaved siblings may feel continued spells of sadness throughout life, although the sadness may not be so intense as time goes on. They may wonder what their sibling would be like now and what the relationship would be like, especially at times of transition in their own lives.

Mental health professionals often give a diagnosis of Dysthymic Disorder to adults who lost a sibling in childhood. This is a long term, low-grade depression. People with dysthymia can go on working but are usually withdrawn and sad and do not live up to their potential. Often other people describe them as having low self-esteem or as being shy. They themselves do not say they are depressed, because they have been that way for so long, it feels natural to them. Many are relieved to discover that this is a treatable condition.

The Missing Piece

Some bereaved siblings possess a "psychic hole" where the sibling used to reside. This hole has a kind of magnetic force that attracts people who were similar to the deceased sibling. Adults often realize that they seek the same type of people over and over, people who remind them of the one they lost.

Jackie: "I was happily married but when I met Dennis, I felt so comfortable around him. I should have noticed that my feelings were way too intense for someone I had just met. I didn't really know him but I was convinced he was just perfect. I felt complete with him, like he filled up that missing piece. Luckily, I realized in time that he reminded me of my older brother, Todd, who died from CF when he was 16. I knew that the wonderful qualities I attributed to Dennis were really those of Todd."

Christie: "My older sister died when she was 17 and I was 12. She had been my mentor all of my life. Now I find that I am drawn to older women—I am always seeking another person to advise me and guide me."

Randy: "My little sister, Ann, was such an angel—blonde, blue eyes, and so petite. I find that I am drawn to women who are younger than me and fit those characteristics—blonde, blue eyed, and petite. The minute I see someone like that, I feel my heart opening up and I think the best of her. Unfortunately, I have been burned a couple of times, because they were not really angels."

I have not been able to find any research on the subject of whether more healing makes this phenomenon disappear. We need to be aware that this curious psychic hole might be operating in our lives so that it does not control us.

Co-dependency

We usually think of co-dependency in relationship to alcohol or drug abuse. However, families that center on an invalid or sick child for a long period of time, develop similar characteristics. Codependents tend to involve themselves in relationships with others who are needy, wounded, or unreliable. The codependent over-functions in the relationship, trying to fill all of the other's needs and desires, but without honoring their own. It is as if they have become so accustomed to having an invalid in their childhood home that they seek out someone to fill that role when they grow up and have their own space.

An unwelcome harvest

It is impossible to list all of the effects that develop over time after the death of a sibling. It is as if a seed has been planted, which grows into a tree and bears fruit. In counseling, survivors learn what characteristics and personality quirks are the fruits of that tree. The fear of loving again, anxiety, a dislike of doctors and hospitals, the inability to finish projects—there are an endless number of ways this loss can affect us. These are all ways that we learned to protect ourselves, and we may not need this kind of protection as adults. It is time to let them go.

Heart-Room

When I first took the measure
of my heart,
I could not see,
the light was dim.
A friend held
the lamp while I looked in.

There was room for someone's sorrow
and another person's pain.
And plenty of room for other people's tears,
that fell like rain.

The depth of my compassion,
everyone could see.
But none of it really mattered until
there was room in my heart
for me.

—P.G. White

7

Creativity and Healing

A ruffled mind makes a restless pillow.

—*Bereaved sibling, Charlotte Bronte*

Many psychologists and researchers have observed the link between creativity and the early loss of a sibling. One of them, George H. Pollock, made a study of creative individuals who had lost siblings during their early lives—people like artists Vincent Van Gogh, Salvador Dali, and Pablo Picasso. Other creative individuals fall into this category, including musicians Elvis Presley, Ray Charles, and Johnny Cash; writers James Barrie (he wrote Peter Pan), Thomas Wolfe, Oscar Wilde, Jack Kerouac, F. Scott Fitzgerald, and Charlotte Bronte.

Pollock thought that creativity could be both the result of resolving grief or part of the grieving process itself, the way that individuals find their balance again after being knocked out of balance by the loss. He believed that children and adolescents did not necessarily become distorted personalities after such a family tragedy. Some of them used the experience in a positive way by becoming creative.

Psychologist Melanie Klein suggested that creativity helps to take the place of the relationship with the lost loved one. She said that drawing and painting could be used to repair a psychological injury. She also notes that not everyone becomes creative in this manner, but becomes more productive in a different way—by becoming capable of the appreciation of life and more tolerant of others—in other words, wiser.

Creativity

- Helps to communicate our feelings about what happened.
- Provides a way to memorialize the dead.
- Offers a means through which the sheer energy of grief can be expended.
- Helps us find meaning in the loss.
- Helps us bridge the worlds between the living and the dead.
- Helps to weaken the power that death has over us.
- Prevents us from forgetting the deceased, at least while we are working on our creation.
- Helps us learn what we have lost.

Some of us try to put our experience into words, through writing or song. Although putting feelings into words may fail to communicate our experience as perfectly as we wish, the simple act of doing it teaches us about what happened. We learn about the nature of love and grief, and form concepts and ideas about it. As we create, what was once vague and formless now begins to take shape in our minds.

Bridging the two worlds

When we create, we attempt to bridge the experience of two worlds—the world of the past when our loved one was with us, and the other world of the present reality, when we have to go on living without them. It may be that when we try to write about the experience, the only words we can find are something like this: "I don't know what to say," "There are no words." "Words fail me." "Words are not adequate to express this sorrow". Words do have value in healing, even when they are used to simply express their inadequacy. Writing helps us to understand the universal mystery of grief, and our unique response.

Memorials

A second kind of creative activity attempts to memorialize the dead person. Some draw or paint, while others create photo albums, scrapbooks, or websites documenting their sibling's life. Others need a larger arena and use gardening or building for their outlet. It keeps our loved one from being forgotten, while we are working on our creation, and afterwards, as a spur to memory. We are not helpless when we create. By creating, we take a stand against the destructive power of death. These imaginative responses to death support us when we need it most.

My Scrapbook Life

For years I have been telling clients to create photo albums and scrapbooks about their lives or the life of their deceased sibling. Last year, I decided it was time for me to take my own advice, so I began making one for myself. It was, at first, a delightful romp down memory lane until, in the book, I reached the age of fifteen, when my sister died.

Suddenly, it was as if an invisible, but powerful force pushed me away from my project. I avoided it for several days, and then decided to skip that page and go around it. I moved ahead to the final page of the book, about my college graduation—and then started working backwards.

For each year, I could see how my sister's death had affected my life. I saw how family became more important to me than ever—I chose my college so I could be near my brother. I realized forcefully how my period of "acting out" in college was a way to escape from pain.

I worked backwards again—back to high school…I saw how my friendships had changed—I gravitated towards more serious students—I was determined to go to college as my sister and I had always planned. I would live for both of us.

Then back to sophomore year…the year that I sang in the church choir. I was not religious, but my sister had been, so after she died, I started going to church. Memories came flooding back, but this time…they were not of sorrow, but of goodness…a classmate who invited me to sing with her at school when I was the new kid…the kindness of adults who took me under their wing and encouraged my dreams…the school counselor who helped me get scholarships…neighbors who talked to me after school. My world was full of loving souls who must have known about my sister's death, and supported me, but I did not realize it at the time.

Then, I went backwards again, to our move from Colorado to California immediately after my sister's funeral. This page in the scrapbook is disjointed and ugly—no matter what I do, I can't seem to fix it. But I realize that it clearly reflects what was going on in my life. Leaving Denver, trying to start over in a new place. We moved to four different houses within that first year—we just couldn't seem to get settled.

And finally, I was back to that difficult page about her death. I sat down to complete the task, but first I reviewed the years before. Looking back at my younger self, I was overwhelmed at my innocence and how naive I had been. It was like seeing someone speeding towards a cliff, totally unaware that they are about to fall into a void.

One of the pictures on the page the year before my sister's death showed me with a horribly frizzy hairstyle. I remember thinking in those days that was the worst thing that could happen to a person—a bad perm. I felt a wave of compassion towards my younger self, who had no way of knowing that her life was about to change forever.

When I finally began to work on the page about my sister, I decided not to make it into a eulogy—the pictures of us together tell exactly what kind of sister she was. There is one photo of her in a pink dress and it is simply labeled as follows: Linda died of a rare form of cancer. She was very religious and believed even at the worst that God was with her. She was artistic, good at sports and music, and loved to read.

My sister's death created ripples into my future but also into my past. I see the time when she was alive as incredibly precious, something to be held close to my heart. I look at her face and imagine that she looks sad, as if she had some premonition of what was about to happen. I see that life does move on whether you agree with what happens or not. Terrible things do happen. You can't ignore them. You can't go around them. But good people do make them easier to bear.

The energy of grief

Grief is a kind of energy and we can use that energy in ways that help to weaken the power death has over us. Although we may be sad while creating, by releasing the sadness in this way, we are in charge, no longer victimized by grief. We are being pro-active rather than re-active—in essence, deliberately calling forth the grief inside, feeling it now so that it doesn't become a burden that weighs us down forever. As we create, we move into the most intimate and personal self, and discover that here, in this private place, we are most connected to all mankind and the universal experience of death.

In our minds, we may be confused and in turmoil. But as we move in to the sheltered regions of the heart, we come to understand our experience and ourselves in a new way.

8

Factors that Influence Sibling Grief

o o o o o o o o o o o o o o o o o o o o o o o o o o o o o o o o

Ever has it been that love knows not its own depth until the hour of separation.

—Bereaved sibling, Kahlil Gibrand

One of the questions I am often asked is: why is my grief so different from that of my other siblings? We have seen the similarities in the reactions of surviving siblings, no matter what their age when the death occurred. But there are significant differences, based on the many factors that influence the grief response.

The Meaning of the Lost Relationship

The particular brother/sister, sister/sister, or brother/brother relationship impacts the intensity of grief. When you lose a sibling, you fit into one of the following relationship categories:

Survivor—older sister/Deceased—younger sister
Survivor—older sister/Deceased—younger brother
Survivor—older brother/Deceased—younger sister
Survivor—older brother/Deceased—younger brother
Survivor—younger sister/Deceased—older sister
Survivor—younger sister/Deceased—older brother
Survivor—younger brother/Deceased—older sister
Survivor—younger brother/Deceased—older brother
Survivor—twin/Deceased—twin

This emphasis on the particular relationship is a factor that may be overlooked, because it seems so obvious. But siblings themselves seem to sense the

68

importance of these categories. When someone tells me they lost a sibling, the first thing they mention is their age and the age of their sibling.

We lose not only our brother or sister, but also our relationship with that person. Each of the relationship categories listed here has its own particular characteristics and took place within a particular environment. A girl, for example (whose father was emotionally distant or physically absent), who loses an older brother, may be losing the only "father" figure she has known. An older sister who loses a young brother may feel as if she is losing her own child.

Kelly writes: "I am eighteen and just witnessed the terrible accidental death of my four year old brother. I still have a semester to go in high school before I graduate. It feels like I just lost my own child. I have taken care of him since his birth, when I was fourteen. How can I ever go back to school?"

When your lost sibling was younger, he or she may have looked up to you and admired you, giving you a boost to your self-esteem. If your sibling was older, he or she may have guided you or provided a role model.

The pain of loss intensifies depending on what the lost relationship meant to you. For adults, whose parents are already deceased, the loss of a particular relationship with a sibling may feel like the loss of all they had left of their parents. If you are the only one left of childbearing age, you may feel obligated to produce grandchildren for your parents. You might be the only one left to carry on the family name or to take over the family business. You are the one who must take responsibility for aging parents. You may be called upon to adopt and care for your sibling's children. It might also mean that there will be no one left to take care of your children if something happens to you.

The world of "what might have been".

When an elderly person dies, we often say, "He (or she) lived a full life." This is because our perception of how fully the deceased person's life was lived makes a great difference in our grief. Thinking about all that they have missed or will never get to experience is painful indeed. We've talked about the world of the living and the world of the dead, but this is the world of "what might have been."

Caleb: "I keep thinking of everything we could have done together, things I wanted to do all my life, but he was too young. We were getting closer and I was looking forward to having him visit me and us growing old together. And now this."

Brigid: "He will never take my kids to a baseball game. He won't get to see them grow up. He was robbed of life, marriage, having kids, family. It's not fair!"

We have a nearly instinctive belief that the oldest people die first and when that doesn't happen, it hurts so much more. When children, teens, or young adults die, we naturally regret all that they have missed.

Preventability is also part of the world of what might have been. When the death could have been prevented, it seems more painful and we can't make sense of it. This issue is particularly poignant for those whose sibling committed suicide. If only our deceased siblings could have talked to us about these problems, we would have helped them work it out. Their death could have been prevented if only they had given us a chance to help. When the cause of death was by some human activity, such as murder or terrorism, it means the death was preventable, and hurts all the more.

What else is going on at the time

When the death of your sibling is one of many crises going on at the same time, the grief process may be complicated. Perhaps a parent's death triggers acting out behavior in a teenage sibling, who is then killed in a drunken car wreck. The death of one family member may trigger suicide in another family member. There may have been a divorce followed by the death of one of the children. It can feel like the whole world is coming apart.

Multiple losses create an overload of stress that we are not built to tolerate. People may respond by becoming numb. Others may grieve only the most significant loss. The "little miracle" that takes place with normal grief (when bereaved individuals wake up one day realizing that life is still going on and that they do want to live) may not occur with multiple losses.

Stress is caused not only by the negative events, but also by positive transitional events of life, such as marriages and the birth of children. This kind of stress also complicates the grief process. What do you do when your sibling dies the day before you are supposed to get married in a large wedding ceremony? What do you feel when your brother dies on the same day your child is born?

There is no good time to lose a brother or sister, but it is harder to accept when they die on your birthday, or Christmas, or the day you were supposed to graduate from college. It is difficult for anyone to tolerate these complicating factors and mixed emotions.

The same, but different

Bereaved siblings often talk about the relief they experience when they discover others who have lost a brother or sister. It makes us feel that we are not alone. Within the population of all those who have shared such a loss, however, there are still differences, and some of those differences make the survivor feel that no one, not even another bereaved sibling, can understand what they are going through. These individuals may need to connect with another person who has experienced almost exactly the same kind of loss in order to banish their sense of isolation.

The following list includes losses that are made more difficult because of the survivor's experience itself or by how they perceive other people will view the death. I want to make it clear that these are not in any kind of order by level of difficulty. Any individual's felt experience of loss is his or her own and cannot be compared to that of another.

- **One brother, sister or other family member murdered another brother or sister or other family member.**

This violation of the family bond is one of the most heinous crimes we can imagine. Surviving siblings in essence lose two loved ones, the victim and the murderer. They and their family may be torn apart by conflicting loyalties. Such an event incorporates other difficulties such as media attention and legal issues, which complicate the loss. Because of the deplorable nature of the crime, survivors may not want anyone to know about it and remain trapped within their grief and shame permanently.

Grief is meant to bring people closer to each other. Where families cannot grieve together, they tend to withdraw from one another, isolating themselves from healing relationships.

- **Where the cause of death was suicide**

In our society, there is still a stigma about suicide. Survivors may not be able to talk easily about what happened. They want to protect both themselves and the memory of their brother or sister from the judgment of other people. Survivors inevitably feel somewhat isolated, especially when other people act embarrassed or uneasy about the cause of death.

- **A surviving sibling accidentally killed a brother or sister.**

This death is most commonly a result of a car accident, where the surviving sibling was driving. Accidental shootings also fall into this group. We know that whenever a sibling dies, there is nearly always an element of guilt involved for survivors. For these particular survivors, however, the natural guilt, which rises from the ambivalent nature of the sibling relationship, is intensified and difficult to overcome. Survivors need to work towards accepting what happened as an accident. Even if they wished their siblings were dead many times during their childhood, that doesn't mean they caused the death. It was still an accident.

Even siblings acting irresponsibly, such as drinking and driving, can eventually find peace. In such cases, acts of atonement may be necessary to satisfy the desire to undo what has happened. The issue of sibling guilt caused by irresponsible behavior is explored in a book written by Anne Tyler, called *Saint Maybe*.

- **The surviving sibling witnessed the death of their brother or sister.**

When a person is traumatized, they feel helpless. Actually witnessing the death of your brother or sister, and not being powerful enough to do anything about it, is devastating. Some individuals have told me that they were not able to accept what they were seeing, so their minds showed them something else. For example, one young girl looked out the window and saw, not her sister being hit and killed by a car, but her sister's friend waving to her and falling off her bike. Years later, as an adult in therapy, when the actual event surfaced, she was able to face the reality of what she had seen.

Others tell me that they saw the death, but "forgot" that they had seen it. Immediately after the event, they had trouble sleeping, and could remember that something had bothered them that day, but they couldn't remember what it was.

Most bereaved siblings are frozen and immobile upon witnessing what happened to their brother or sister. But as time goes by, they begin to wonder why they didn't do anything to help. When they talk about it, and someone asks,

"Couldn't you do anything to help?" they feel terrible, and blame themselves even more. The movie, *Ray*, about the life of Ray Charles, gives an artistic, but emotionally accurate portrayal of the kind of psychological disturbance that can be caused by witnessing such an event.

- **When the death is surrounded by a lot of media attention**

Deaths caused by murder or mass tragedy, such as 9/11, mining disasters, or plane crashes cannot be grieved in private. They usually involve additional factors such as legal issues that delay the resolution of grief. Wherever the mourners go, people are talking about the event that killed their sibling. Attention from the media adds stress to already overstressed survivors. When the deceased was already a public figure, survivors must risk seeing their grief on the 9 o'clock news.

Summary

Since individuals differ, their grief and mourning will differ. There are numerous factors that account for some of the differences. We tend to suffer more when we believe that our sibling's life was unfulfilled and we have more difficulty when there are already other troubling events going on around us. When we have actually witnessed the death, we may need to deal first with the shock and trauma before we can deal with the loss. When the cause of death is perceived as shameful or we have to hide from media attention, we may not be able to reach out for support.

9

Memories, Dreams, and Ongoing Connections

o o o o o o o o o o o o o o o o o o o o o o o o o o o o o o o o o o

"Death is nothing at all. It does not count.
I have only slipped into another room."

—*Henry Scott Holland*

This chapter is about the connections between ourselves and our deceased siblings. Experts in grief once told us that, in order to resolve grief, we had to give up our connection with the deceased and move on into life.

I wanted to explore this idea of a "connection" with a deceased loved one, so I designed a research study to compare two groups of bereaved siblings: one group who said they still had an ongoing connection with their deceased sibling, and one group who said they did NOT have such a connection. Both groups had to be equal in size. I discovered that it was almost impossible to find enough people for the second group—those who did NOT have such a connection.

After interviewing the people in the NOT connected group, I had the feeling that eventually, after enough healing had taken place, they would "re-connect" with their deceased sibling.

This discovery led me to question the earlier theories of grief stages, and I now believe that the connection between surviving siblings and deceased siblings is ongoing, and this connection is perceived as a good thing, which does not prevent survivors from moving on into life.

Some of the ways in which bereaved siblings experience a connection with their brother or sister is by:

- Thinking about them

- Talking about them

- Participating in activities once shared with the deceased

- Engaging in the deceased sibling's interests or concerns

- Creating memorials—these can be small, such as a donation of flowers to the church on their birthday, or large, like naming a building for them.

- Remembering them during life transitions (graduations, re-locations, weddings, funerals…)

- Treasuring objects linked to the deceased in some way.

- Keeping their photo nearby or in the survivor's wallet

- Dreaming about them

A Psychic Connection?

In one study at the Sibling Connection, we asked bereaved siblings whether they had experienced any psychic or supernatural phenomena around the time of their sibling's death. Bereaved siblings often mention such events.

Some of the most common are:

- Dreams foretelling or warning of the death

- "Poltergeist" events associated with the deceased

- Hearing the voice of the deceased just before the death

- Seeing a glimpse of the sibling after their death

- Feeling the presence of the deceased at crucial times in the life of the surviving sibling.

- Even decades later, when another loss occurs, feeling the deceased sibling as being nearby, offering comfort.

- Noticing objects or events that remind them of the deceased

Warning dreams were the most common phenomena that I heard about during my research. Some dreams of this type are not necessarily about the death of the sibling, but warn that the world as known is coming to an end.

Poltergeist events described by surviving siblings are simple events that have meaning for the bereaved. For example, the survivor comes home from the funeral and finds the sibling's graduation photo lying face down on the floor where it fell from the end table. A missing piece of jewelry or object belonging to the deceased is found in an unlikely spot.

Sara's story: "My brother always called me Scooter—that was his nickname for me. I liked it because he was the only one who used it. I had a scooter when I was a kid, but it had been lost for years. A few days after Gary died, I was in the basement, and there was my scooter, right out in the open, where no one could miss it! I felt like it was a message from Gary, telling me that he was OK."

Some bereaved siblings hear the voice of their brother or sister calling to them immediately before the death. The survivor perceives this phenomenon as a farewell or a reaching out at the moment of death. Some see the deceased sibling where they would expect to see them, and then realize that it was not possible.

Karen's story: "I looked out the window and I could swear I saw my sister swinging in the backyard swing. But just then the doorbell rang and the police came to the door and we learned that she had just been hit by a bus and killed two hours earlier."

Some survivors describe incidents in which they experienced "a presence", like an angel or spirit near them. This might occur at a time when the survivor was feeling suicidal or in danger. The presence is perceived as helpful and loving.

Siblings tell me that psychic phenomena are comforting and are meant to reassure them that there is a spiritual world and that they will see their sibling some time in an after life. Most psychic events take place near to the time of death. Not every surviving sibling experiences such phenomena. But many do, and it is important for them to know they are not alone in feeling connected at this psychic depth.

Dreams

Much of my clinical work is with bereaved siblings who often talk in the first session about a disturbing dream. I soon realized that there are patterns to these dreams, common to many adults bereaved when they were young.

Typical dreams (All dreams used here with permission)

Daniel (his brother died at age 8): "I am in an attic and look around at all the old toys from childhood. Everything is dusty and gray. I see a chest in the corner, walk over, and open the lid. Inside I see my brother, sitting there as if waiting for someone. I don't know how he could be small enough to be inside the chest, but it is as if he has been waiting for me to find him. He doesn't say anything, but just patiently waits there. I hadn't even thought about him for years."

Marilynne: "I am looking for something I lost. We have an old storage room off the garage, and in the dream I go up to the door, but hesitate to go in. Finally, I open the door and turn on the light. Everything is all lined up on shelves and in boxes on the floor. My brother, who has been dead for at least 20 years, is sitting on one of the shelves, just quietly waiting there. He doesn't seem to notice me, he just looks very patient."

These dreams are understandably upsetting, and after time in therapy, the dreams change.

Daniel's second dream: "I walk into the kitchen of my house and my brother is there, eating lunch and getting ready to go play baseball. He seems happy, smiling at me and telling me about his game."

This dream sequence seems to imply that an important part of the dreamer's life had been shut away, and needed to be brought into the dreamer's everyday life. It was difficult for Daniel to begin talking about his brother, but once he did, his demeanor brightened considerably. As he talked more and more about his early life, of which his brother was so much a part, he became more animated and seemed younger.

Repetitive Dreams

Another kind of dream that brings individuals into therapy is the repetitive dream (or nightmare) related to the trauma of the sibling's death. It is as if the dream-making part of the brain is trying to work through the trauma, but not quite succeeding.

Carl, a chef in training: "I am getting out the pans to create a dish for my final exam. I turn to the sink, and there is my brother, very tiny, drowning in the sink. The last time I had this dream, he was drowning at the pool where my kids go in the summer." The circumstances are somewhat different, because his ten-year-old brother died by drowning while boating, but clearly the dream is working through this event. It also seems to imply that something about his brother's death is getting in the way of succeeding in his chosen career.

Suzie: "In the dream I am a concert pianist. There is a huge audience, and I am about ready to start playing. I go to the piano and open the bench to take out my music. But there in the bench is my sister, who died when she was 3 years old and I was 9. She got trapped in an old refrigerator and suffocated. In the dream she is alive, but it looks like I opened the bench just in time to keep her from suffocating."

Because of the frequency with which clients brought in dreams of deceased siblings, I carried out a survey of 68 individuals, all bereaved siblings. The dreams fell into the following categories:

1.) Dreams that foretell the death in some way

Alicia: "In my dream I saw a golden line of light hovering in the air above me—then it kind of turned into my older brother. He told me clearly that he was leaving now and asked me to take care of my mother. The dream was so realistic I woke up and called my sister, and she had just had a similar dream! It was later in the day we found out my brother had died of a heart attack at the age of 33."

Richard: "On the day my brother died, I woke up from a dream that the world was in ruins, everywhere I looked all the familiar landmarks were knocked down, just rubble all over. I woke up feeling scared and then got the phone call that changed me forever."

2.) Dreams in which the deceased sibling is still alive and everything is normal

Mark: "I dreamed that my brother and I were little kids playing old 45 records. We were just having fun. I woke up feeling so happy until I remembered that he had died.

3.) Dreams in which the deceased sibling is still alive, but in which the dreamer realizes that the sibling is supposed to be dead.

Christi: "I went into the basement in my dream and my brother was just sitting there watching television. I say to him—I thought you were dead and he just laughs at me, like it's a joke."

4.) Dreams in which the deceased sibling comforts the surviving sibling

Pam: "In my dream I am searching for something in a room with all kinds of old furniture, like in a movie—I think it might have been jewels. Suddenly my brother appears and I am surprised and tell him that I thought he was dead, and he should come home now. He looks at me sadly and says—I'm sorry, I can't go with you."

5.) Repetitive dreams, usually repeating the traumatic aspect of the death

Todd's brother died in a car accident and he suffered for a long time with variations of the following dream: "I am watching TV when the news comes on telling about a car accident and I just know that it is my brother. I switch off the TV and go outside and suddenly I am at the high school where they have a banged up car out in front to warn the kids about drunken driving. I realize it is Justin's car and I feel sick and wake up."

6.) Dreams in which the dreamer makes a decision to go on living and wakes up feeling guilty about this.

Lisa: (her brother died in an automobile accident at 19) "I am with my kids at the park when a policeman comes up to me and tells me that my brother has been hurt in a car accident and needs me to come. I look over and see my kids up on the climbing frame. One of them is scared and frozen and I know that I have to rescue her. I say to the policeman—I'm sorry; I have to take care of my kids. I woke up feeling so guilty but then later that day I came across a picture of me and my brother at the park and I felt like he was saying that he understood and wanted me to go on living."

7.) Dreams in which the sibling appears somewhere unexpected.

Often, in these dreams, the deceased sibling is found in a place which is usually unused or where objects are stored, such as closets, basements, or attics. There is no sense of distress, but a sense of the sibling patiently waiting to be found. Sometimes the dreamer discovers the sibling just before they are to go onstage or engage in some important activity.

8.) Repetitive dreams that last for years and then come to some kind of conclusion

The most compelling of all the dream types are those that come to some kind of resolution, after years of repetition. In them, there are first the repetitive dreams, then dreams that signal a change has taken place, and finally a resurrection and recognition dream that surprises and comforts the dreamer.

1.) Katie's dream sequence

"Shortly after Hallie's death I dreamed that I looked in the junk room where we did ironing, and there was Hallie in her hospital bed. I rushed out and told Mom that Hallie wasn't dead, she was just sleeping in the storage room—I was so happy. As the years went by I continued to have this dream with some variations. The next time I had it, I drove to the hospital and found her in her hospital bed. Each time I had the dream, I had to drive further and further away and the dreams were separated by years and even decades.

Finally, when my kids were ten and 6, I had the dream again. This time I drove for a long, long time and when finally arrived at my destination, I had to walk down long, long corridors. Finally, I saw doors at the end of the hall. As I approached I saw two nurses at the door. They opened the door for me and I saw Hallie there in her hospital bed with all the tubes in her arms. The nurses looked at me compassionately. One said "Can't you let her go?" At that moment I realized that it was me causing her to still be there in the bed. I was ashamed of myself—I bowed my head in shame. I knew that I had to do something so that she could be released from the trauma. When I woke up, I called and made an appointment to see you."

Subsequently, Katie had the following dream: "I dreamed I was shopping with two little girls, one was me as a child and one was Hallie, and suddenly I realized they weren't with me and I was scared at first, but then I thought what a relief it was to have them gone—now I could accomplish something. I went on doing my shopping, but woke up feeling overwhelmed with guilt." Later still, she had the following dream: "I am looking through a photo album which is all black and white photos, except one of Hallie wearing a green dress."

And finally, a dream of resurrection and recognition: "I am at the mall shopping when I suddenly realize that I am not alone. There is another woman with me. I look at her and don't know who she is. Then she speaks to me and I suddenly recognize her as my sister, all grown up like me." I wake up feeling wonderful—comforted, whole, at peace with the world."

2.) Robert's dream sequence

"My sister Laura was in a wheelchair for years before she died. Immediately afterwards I started having this repeating dream where I would look into her room and there would be her empty wheelchair. Sometimes it would change and I would be at school going to class and there was this empty wheelchair near my locker, but I knew it was hers because she had a little teddy bear hanging on it. I always woke up feeling bad because it reminded me that she was gone."

Years later, Robert had the following dream. "I am in a house that I don't recognize, and I go into a room that seems familiar and there is the empty wheelchair, but the teddy bear is gone. But then I notice it is sitting on a shelf with other toys and books. I remember thinking that Laura was pretty organized to have her toys all lined up like that."

Later, in real life, after Robert had grown and had children of his own, his mother died. He had the following dream: "I am at home but taking my girls somewhere. They go out to wait in the car, but I sense that there is still someone else in the house. Then I see a girl standing there and I have no idea who she is. She comes up and hugs me and I suddenly realize that it is Laura, but she is much older than when she died. I know that she is comforting me about Mom's death. When I woke up I felt so much better. It was so good to know that I wasn't alone—that she was still there for me, even after death."

Robyn's dream sequence

"My brother was killed in a car accident, at a place where the road curves and there is a deep embankment by the road. In my dream, I am biking along that road and suddenly I see a monster about ready to come up out of the embankment. I wake up terrified. I had that dream for years, and I woke up each time with my heart thundering."

After time in therapy, Robyn had the following dream: "I am biking along the road and it's getting dark and I sense a presence coming towards me, all shadowy. I start to turn and ride away but I hear my brother calling me to stop. Suddenly, the shadows fade and I can see my brother clearly. He tells me that he wasn't trying to scare me. He just wanted me to know he was there. All that time I thought it was something terribly frightening, but it was him all along."

The fact that dreams of deceased siblings go on for so long after the death indicate the connection is still there, whether or not we think of them consciously. The survivor siblings who shared these dreams all made a similar observation. They said that at first they felt like part of them died with their sibling. After the recognition dream, however, they realized for the first time that part of their sibling lived on in them. I call these dreams "resurrection and recognition" dreams because the dreamers seem to undergo a rebirth of part of their personality at about the same time that they have the dream.

Connecting through Memories

Some siblings are afraid that they will forget their brother or sister, and rightly so. Although they will never forget what their sibling meant to them, specific memories do fade. Creating some kind of memory store is important in the early weeks after the death of a sibling. Even if many years have passed, however, it is never too late to begin.

While there are many ways to capture memories, such as making videos, these have to be done in advance. When siblings die without warning, we have to work harder to preserve our memories. The activity of creating a memory store, such as a photo album or scrapbook, is healing in itself. Not everything fits into a book, however, so bigger items can be stored in a memory box and filled with linking objects.

Linking objects

Linking objects are any tangible objects that remind you of the person who died. They can be articles of clothing, or any belonging that you associate with the deceased, such as a toy, favorite book, or piece of jewelry. Photos and letters can be linking objects and bereaved siblings may carry a photograph with them at all times. They may fear that they will forget how their sibling looked, and photos help them remember. This is not macabre behavior; it is normal to want to be close to our sibling's belongings when we can't have the actual person with us.

Creating a Memory Box

Step 1

Find the right box. A memory box can be any box, from a shoebox to an expensive inlaid wooden box. Decorate it if you wish.

Step 2

Gather together items you treasure because they belonged to or remind you of your brother or sister, even something you wrote about them. This might include treasured toys, yearbooks, letters from them, emails, video or audiocassettes, report cards, and photographs.

Step 3

Then, using whatever technology with which you are familiar, record yourself (or your child, if you are a parent reading this) talking about each of the objects. Say what the object is and then tell why you included it. Talk about any memories that it brings to mind. "This is the silver dollar that we found on the parking lot at the grocery store. We were going to split the money but we decided to save it. That was the day we spent over at Uncle Danny's pool." "This is a picture of our vacation at Disneyland; oh, it was so cool! I never want to forget that trip—Jeff was so excited and happy. I'm glad to remember him being so happy."

Have someone ask questions to elicit more information about each object, to get you (or your child) talking. When you are finished, put the tape cassette or CD into the memory box. In later years, you will be glad for the time you spent doing this. No matter what your age at the time of your sibling's death, recording your own voice adds another dimension to your memories. If you are a parent helping your child with this exercise, he or she will thank you in the future for creating this time capsule.

Other Rituals

As time passes, bereaved siblings may wish to engage in other activities to keep the connection with their deceased sibling. Some write letters to their siblings, visit their grave, have their sibling's favorite meal on their birthdays, listen to their music, and hold special candlelight memorials.

Several national support organizations organize memorials and facilitate keeping the connection. They welcome bereaved siblings to their meetings:

Bereaved Parents of the USA 708-748-7866

The Compassionate Friends 877-969-0010

Parents of Murdered Children, Inc. 888-818-POMC

American Foundation for Suicide Prevention 212-363-3500

10

Bibliotherapy for Survivor Siblings of all ages

o o o o o o o o o o o o o o o o o o o o o o o o o o o o o o o

In all things it is better to hope than to despair.

—*Bereaved sibling, Johann Wolfgang von Goethe*

In this final chapter, I want to provide readers a way to help themselves with their own healing. Bibliotherapy means using the reading of books as a way to heal ourselves, gain insight, or solve a problem. Although it is often associated with "self-help" books, any kind of book, fiction or nonfiction, can be used. Bibliotherapy is a dynamic process, by which I mean that we meet the author in the pages of the book. As we read, a dialog begins to take place between the reader and the author. We interpret what we read in light of our own experiences, and thus become a part of the book. The use of movies (cinematherapy) is a similar process.

One of the most troublesome results of losing a sibling is that we feel powerless. In a flash, our power is robbed from us. Reading and actively using bibliotherapy can help us get some of that power back. As we gather information, identify language and feelings that define what happened to us, we begin to gain some mastery of the experience. Our attempt to understand what we read and to compare and contrast it to our experience creates new, hopefully beneficial ways of thinking and feeling.

Adults who lost a sibling in childhood or adolescence find bibliotherapy to be particularly helpful, by selecting books written for adults as well as those written for young readers, the age they were when the death occurred. Non-fiction books (like the one you are reading now) provide a cognitive structure, or way of understanding, what happened when our siblings died.

For survivor siblings, some of the benefits can be to:

- Give us a vocabulary about the subject of sibling grief and sibling loss
- Gather information about sibling loss in general
- Help us work through our experiences by giving us an opportunity to compare and contrast our experiences with those described in the book.
- Help us identify and name our feelings about the loss.
- Reduce our feelings of isolation as we recognize characters who remind us of ourselves.
- Give us a sense of perspective about the level of resources and support available to us at the time of the loss.
- Let us "go back in time" by observing a character who is the age that we were at the time of our sibling's death.
- Help us see that our negative emotions, such as jealousy and guilt, are normal.
- Let us see how the loss impacted others, which we may have missed if we were numb after the loss.
- Learn how other bereaved siblings adjusted to the loss.
- Make it easier for us to tell our stories, and to place the experience of loss within the story of our lives.
- Provide catharsis, or the release of buried emotions.
- Encourage insight and self-awareness.
- Help break up stagnant ways of thinking about our experiences.
- Stimulate our own creativity

One difference between simply reading and bibliotherapy is that of intent. You purposely choose the book because you believe it may solve a problem or facilitate healing. Since you are practicing bibliotherapy instead of just reading the book, follow these four basic steps:

1. **Hoping and wondering**
2. **Reading**
3. **Evaluating**

4.　**Creating**

Hoping and Wondering

The first step is an attitude of hopefulness and curiosity. Surviving siblings are often angry with parents and other authorities who failed them when their sibling died. Consequently, they may discount any suggestion that comes from an authority, such as the idea that reading a book can be helpful. Some surviving siblings spend years trying to "get the best" of authorities by proving them wrong. As much as you can, try to let go of that attitude while you carry out this exercise. To benefit from bibliotherapy, it is necessary to have an open mind.

Reading

Step two is to read the book. Most of the books listed on the booklist are available from local libraries or bookstores. Try to find time when you won't be disturbed. Then read the book, taking notes if necessary.

Evaluating

Step three is the most important part of the exercise. Think about what you have read and give it some time to sink in. Then talk about it with a therapist, spouse, parent, sibling, or trusted friend. Evaluate the book from the point of view of the story of the loss AND as a piece of written material. You may, for example, find the surviving sibling's story to be thought provoking, even though you think the writing is terrible. You may have enjoyed the inspired language in the book, and yet found the story of loss to be unrealistic. With your listener there to support you, compare and contrast the story with your experience, and ask yourself what you have learned from the book.

If you like, use the guidelines here during the evaluating phase, by completing the following sentences and adding others:

1.　Before I read the book, I hoped_____.

2.　The character with whom I identified most was _____ because_____.

3.　The way the character learned about the death was _____.

4.　The way I learned about my sibling's death was_____.

5.　In the first hour after learning of the death, the character_____.

6. In the first hour after learning of my sibling's death, I_____.

7. My experience of loss differed from that of the surviving sibling in the book because_____.

8. My experience of loss was like that of the surviving sibling in the book because_____.

9. The way the surviving sibling (and the family) in the book changed as a result of the loss was_____.

10. The way I changed (and my family) after our loss was_____.

11. Now that I realize how young (innocent, naïve) I was at the time of the loss, I_____.

12. I'm sorry that_____.

13. I wish that _____.

14. Talking to you about this feels_____.

Creating

Finally, try to bring some closure to your work with the book, perhaps by a creative effort of your own, such as drawing, painting, or writing. If you can't think of any ideas for this stage, use one of these.

1. Even if you stopped drawing at the age of 8, draw a picture related to the book, or to your own experience. Use callouts (comic strip balloons) and put in what you were thinking or what you said.

2. Make a list of words that described your feelings about the book and make them into a poem.

3. Make a collage from magazine pictures to illustrate some aspect of your experience.

4. Write a letter to the author of the book and tell him or her about your story and how the book connected to it. I hope that some of you will write to me at the Sibling Connection and tell me how your story connected to this book. The site is located at **www.siblingconnection.net.**

Caution: *This kind of grief work may bring unresolved feelings to the surface. Make sure you have emotional support available to you when you undertake bibliotherapy.*

If you are ready to get started, go on to the booklist and find yourself a book!

Book List

Books about the death of an infant sibling

All Shining in the Spring: The Story of a Baby Who Died by Siobhan Parkinson
The author wrote this for her 6-year-old son when his baby brother died at birth.

Am I Still a Sister? by Alicia M. Sims
An 11-year-old girl loses her 13-month-old brother. For young children. Not to be confused with the next book, with a similar title.

Am I Still a Big Sister? by Audrey Bernheimer Weir
A young girl talks about her feelings when her baby sister gets sick and dies.

Anna's Scrapbook: Journal of a Sister's Love by Susan Aitken
A young girl loses her baby sister. For very young children.

Baby by Patricia MacLachlan J/F grades 4-6
This is the story of Larkin, a 12-year-old girl, whose parents had lost a baby boy that Larkin never knew. When they find an infant on their doorstep, they take care of her for a year, which forces them to deal with the earlier loss. Shows the impact that the loss of a sibling can have, even when that brother or sister has not been known.

The Baby Project by Sarah Ellis J/F 4-6
11-year-old Jessica is excited about getting a new baby sister. When the baby dies suddenly from SIDS, however, her joy is plunged into sorrow. Also published as The Family Project, it shows how her family deals with loss.

Belle Pruitt by V. Cleaver J/F 4-6
Set in Florida, the story of an 11-year-old girl, whose baby brother died of pneumonia, and how she copes with this loss.

Dancing on the Moon by Janice Roper
When her little brother dies, 5-year-old Carly dreams of going to the moon to get him back. She learns that he is always with her in her heart.

Getting Near to Baby by Audrey Couloumbis J/F 4-6
When their infant sister dies and their mother becomes depressed, 12-year-old Willa Jo and her little sister, who has been mute since the death, are taken to live with their Aunt Patty. The children climb on the roof to get closer to their baby sister. Shows how bereaved siblings can also lose their parents emotionally, when parents cannot care for them because of the parents' own grief.

Last Week My Brother Anthony Died by Martha Hickman
A little girl describes her feelings about the death of her 4-week-old baby brother from congenital heart disease and what it is like to lose someone before you really get to know them.

Loving Ben by Elizabeth Laird J/F 7-9
Teenage Anna experiences the birth and death of her hydrocephalic brother, and learns about life and love.

Last Week My Brother Anthony Died by Martha Hickman
A little girl describes her feelings about the death of her 4-week-old baby brother from congenital heart disease and what it is like to lose someone before you really get to know them.

Molly's Rosebush by Janice Cohn J/F 1-2
Molly is expecting a new baby, but it isn't strong enough to be born. She and her family find ways to express their grief and help each other.

Morgan's Baby Sister: A Read-Aloud Book for Families Who Have Experienced the Death of a Newborn by Pauline Johnson J/F 1-2
Morgan is excited about the birth of a new baby, but the baby dies, and she tries to understand her feelings.

My Always Sister Coloring Book
Available from The Centering Corporation
Big sister Callie loses her just born sister Laura. For very young children.

No New Baby: For Siblings Who Have a Brother or Sister Die Before Birth by Marilyn Gryte
For young children (primary and pre-school) who experience the death of a sibling before it is born.

Remembering Our Baby by Patti Keough
A workbook for children whose brother or sister died before it was born. Pre-school.

Stacy Had a Little Sister by Wendie Old J/F 1-2
Stacy had a lot of feelings about her new sister Ashley, but when Ashley dies of SIDS, Stacy misses her.

Where's Jess by Joy and Marv Johnson
For a young child who loses a brother, but doesn't really understand what death is.

You Take the High Road by Mary K. Pershall J/F 7-9
Set in Australia, this tells the story of teenage Samantha, and the loss of her baby brother.

Death of a Sibling During Childhood

Adeline Street by Carol Lynch Williams J/F 4-6
This is a year in the life of 12-year-old Leah, in which she learns to move on after the death of her younger sister, Kelly, who died suddenly from an aneurysm.

Artie's Brief: The Whole Truth, and Nothing But by Christi Killien J/F 4-6
Twelve-year-old Artie is trying to cope with the suicide of his older brother. Artie wants to become a lawyer. He decides to take on the case of an unpopular schoolmate who he feels has had the same unfair deal in life that his brother had.

Beat the Turtle Drum by Constance C. Greene J/F 4-6
Thirteen-year-old Kate grows up quickly when her beloved younger sister, Joss, falls out of a tree and dies. She becomes acquainted with a wide range of feelings as she learns to cope with her loss.

A Birthday Present for Daniel by Juliet Rothman J/F 4-6
A little girl's brother has died and she tells the story of his loss and her feelings afterwards. This book addresses the issue of what to do about the birthday of the dead child.

Drive-By by Lynne Ewing J/F 4-6
Tito's older brother has been killed in a drive-by shooting.

Eighty-Eight Steps to September: A Novel Jan Marino J/F 4-6
Eleven-year-old Amy fights and plays with her 13-year-old brother Robbie like any sister. When he is hospitalized with leukemia, she stubbornly believes he will come home. Before he dies, she is able to fulfill his final wish.

Fig Pudding Ralph Fletcher J/F 4-6
Eleven-year-old Cliff is the oldest in the family. Life for him is a mixture of conflict, excitement and tragedy, when his brother, Brad, dies.

Flapjack Waltzes Nancy Hope Wilson J/F 4-6
Ten-year-old Natalie's younger brother was killed in a car accident. Two years later, she still struggles with the loss. An elderly neighbor helps her to understand loss and the connection between them helps her move on with life.

Ghost Brother C. Adler J/F 4-6
Fifteen-year-old Jon-O was killed in an accident, but his spirit appears to his 12-year-old brother Wally, encouraging him to be more daring. Wally still seeks his brother's approval, and gets it when he is able to move on into life.

Home from Far Jean Little J/F 4-6
When Missy was 10 years old, her twin brother Michael was killed in an automobile accident. A year later, her parents decide to take in two foster children, one of them called Michael. Missy is afraid her parents are trying to forget her twin.

Kelly and Me by Carol Lynch Williams J/F 4-6
Eleven-year-old Leah struggles with the sudden death of her 10-year-old sister, Kelly, from an aneurysm.

Lanky Longlegs by Karin Lorentzon J/F 4-6
Nine-year-old Di experiences both life and death in this book, when her brother dies and her dog has puppies. Explores the meaning of loss.

Last Left Standing by Barbara T. Russell J/F 4-6
Thirteen-year-old Josh struggles after the sudden death of his older brother, Toby. He pretends that his brother is not dead. After connecting to some friends of his brother, Josh gains the strength to face the truth.

Little Women by Louisa May Alcott J/F 4-6 Also a film with the same name.
A story of four sisters: Meg, Jo, Amy, and Beth. When Beth dies, Jo finds comfort in self-expression through writing. Semi-autobiographical.

Lone Wolf by Kristine Franklin J/F 4-6
Three years ago 11-year-old Perry's little sister died in a car accident. His parents divorce and he is living with his father in an isolated area. A family moves in nearby and he gradually makes friends with the oldest girl, Willow. Through his relationship with her and her family, he begins to open his heart again.

Magic Moth by Virginia Lee J/F 4-6
Ten-year-old Maryanne dies, leaving her brother, six-year-old Mark-O and the rest of her family grieving, but able to gain wisdom about loss.

Mick Harte Was Here by Barbara Parks J/F 4-6
Thirteen-year-old Phoebe struggles with the improbable death of her fun-loving brother, 12-year-old Mick, in a bicycle accident.

My Brother Joey Died by G. McLendon J/F 4-6
Shows what grief is like for children from the viewpoint of a little girl whose brother dies.

My Brother's Ghost by Allan Ahlberg J/F 4-6
Narrator Frances looks back on her life to a time after her 10-year-old brother Tom was killed in an accident. His ghost returns as a guardian to the 9-year-old Frances and in time she comes to terms with his death.

My twin sister Erika by Ilse-Margaret Vogel J/F 4-6
Inge questions her own identity after the death of her sister.

Nobody's Fault by Patricia Hermes J/F 4-6
Emily likes her brother Matthew but is annoyed by his teasing. She thinks it is her fault when he dies in a freak accident. She is helped by visits to a psychiatrist.

Run, Run, As Fast As You Can by Mary Pope Osborne J/F 4-6
Eleven-year-old Hallie has moved around a lot. But at least she always has her brother, Michael, to be her friend. When her family moves to Virginia, however, she is devastated by his death, made worse by her parents' hiding information.

Searching for David's Heart by Cherie Bennett Ages 9-12
Darcy's older brother, David, died in an accident, and Darcy believed it was her fault because of a fight they had just before the accident. David's heart is used in a transplant, and when she meets the boy who got David's heart, she learns a powerful lesson about life.

Snowdrops for Cousin Ruth by Susan Katz J/F 4-6
Nine-year-old Johanna can still hear the voice of her younger brother, Johnnie, who was killed when a car skidded out of control while he and his twin sister, Susie, were building a snowman. Susie stops speaking completely. An elderly relative comes to live nearby and they begin to heal.

The Soul of the Silver Dog by Lynn Hall J/F 4-6
Feeling withdrawn and alienated after her younger sister's death from cystic fibrosis, teenaged Cory adopts a blind show dog and is determined to bring back some of his earlier glory.

Stone Orchard by Susan Merritt History Grade 4 and up
Set in Canada in 1866, this is the story of fourteen-year-old Maud Fraser, who is troubled by the sudden death of her little brother. She thinks her father blames her for the child's death. When her village is taken over after a battle, she turns her home into a field hospital, and takes care of the wounded. She learns a family secret and the truth about her brother's sudden death.

Tawny by Chas Carner J/F 4-6
Twelve-year-old Trey Landry is trying to come to terms with the death of his twin brother. He adopts and takes care of an injured doe.

Writing to Richie by Patricia Calvert J/F 4-6
David and his younger brother, Richie, are foster children who have finally found some good parents. They are happy until Richie dies suddenly from an anaphylactic reaction. The foster parents get a new child, Ollie, who helps David learn to live with his loss.

Beyond Silence by Eleanor Cameron J/F 7-9
Fifteen-year-old Andy tries to live in the moment, and not look back into the past. But he is disturbed by a recurring dream after his brother Hoagy's death. He goes to Scotland with his father and encounters one of his ancestors.

Calling the Swan by Jean Thesman J/F 7-9
This is the story of Skylar, whose older sister, Alexandra, was abducted, and presumed murdered, when she went to the lake to feed the swans. The story shows how the cause of death impacts siblings. Friends stopped coming over, and she is understandably over-protected by her parents. As she begins to make friends in summer school, Skylar begins to heal.

Carolina Autumn by Carol Lynch Williams J/F 7-9
Fourteen-year-old Carolina has suffered a terrible loss, both of her older sister and her father. She is struggling to cope and learns to express her feelings.

Chinese Handcuffs by Chris Crutcher Fiction Young Adult
Still troubled by guilt about his older brother's violent suicide, eighteen-year-old Dillon becomes involved with Jennifer, drawn to her and connected by the pain they have both experienced.

Dead Birds Singing by Marc Talbot J/F 7-9
Twelve year old Matt loses both his mother and later his sister in a car accident. He has to go and live with a friend and come to terms with the tragedy.

Del-Del by Victor Kelleher Fiction ages 12 and up
A horror story in which Beth tells of her older sister's death and the impact it has on 7-year-old Sam, who becomes possessed by an evil creature called Del-Del.

How Could You Do It, Diane? by Stella Pevsner (death of stepsister) J/F 7-9
When her 15-year-old stepsister commits suicide, 14-year-old Bethany is left with questions that plague her. Shows how the parents' attempt to keep quiet about what happened delays and confuses her grief process.

I Miss You, I Miss You! by Peter Pohl J/F 7-9
Thirteen-year-old Tina is shocked by the death of her identical twin, Cilla, who is hit by a car on the way to school. Gradually she learns to live with the loss.

Liza's Star Wish by Diana Stevens J/F 7-9
Fourteen-year-old Liza has to spend the summer with her grandmother and doesn't like it. However, it is here she learns how to cope with the drowning of her younger sister, Holly. The author explores how cremation and the lack of a grave affect her.

Many Stones by Carolyn Coman J/F 7-9
Sixteen-year-old Berry tries to come to terms with the murder, a year earlier, of her sister Laura in South Africa. She and her father travel there to dedicate a memorial.

Memory by Margaret Mahy J/F 7-9
Nineteen-year-old Johnny is still troubled by guilt about the death of his younger sister, Janine, who fell off a cliff five years earlier. He feels responsible, and searches for the only other witness to the event.

Mourning Song by Lurlene McDaniel Fiction YA
Dani's older sister Cassie has a brain tumor, and Dani is determined to fulfill her sister's last wish before she dies.

My Brother Has AIDS by Deborah Davis J/F 7-9
When her 27-year-old brother, Jack, comes home to die from AIDS, 13-year-old Lacy has to come to grips with his illness and impending death, and the social stigma of AIDS.

My Brother Sam Is Dead by James Lincoln Collier J/F 7-9
This is the story of Tim Meeker, whose 16 year-old brother, Sam Meeker, goes to fight in the Revolutionary War and ends up being killed.

My Brother Stealing Second by Jim McNaughton J/F 7-9
Sixteen-year-old Bobby tries to come to terms with his grief about the death of his brother, Billy, in a car accident, and the way other people react to it.

My Daniel by Pam Conrad J/F 7-9
Two children, Ellie and Stevie, go to the museum with their grandmother, Julia, who tells them stories of her brother's search for dinosaur bones. Julia was 12 when her older brother Daniel was struck by lightning and killed. Telling the story to her grandchildren, Julia finds a new perspective on her loss.

The Other Shepards by Adele Griffin J/F 7-9
Teenage Holland and her younger sister, Geneva, were born after the tragic death of three older siblings, a girl and two boys, in a car accident. They are haunted by this event, their identities defined by the loss. Annie, possibly a ghost, arrives and their lives begin to change. They travel to the island where the other Shepards died, and begin to re-create themselves, apart from the grief and memories of the siblings they had never known.

Phoenix Rising: Or How to Survive Your Life by Cynthia D. Grant J/F 7-9
When her 18-year-old sister Helen dies of cancer, Jessie (Helen's younger sister) begins reading Helen's journal. As the story unfolds, moving between Helen's journal entries and Jessie's telling of the story, the reader is drawn into Helen's struggle with dying and Jessie's struggle with staying alive.

Probably Still Nick Swansen: A Novel by Virginia Euwer Wolff J/F 7-9
Sixteen-year-old Nick struggles everyday because of his learning disability. Nick is also troubled by the memory of watching his older sister drown.

Remembering Mog by Colby Rodowsky J/F 7-9
Annie is about ready to graduate from high school. She remembers back two years ago when her sister, Mog, was shot and killed just before her graduation. Shows the range of emotion and defenses of family members.

Signs of Life by Jean Ferris Young Adult
Seventeen-year-old Hannah is struggling with grief over the death of her twin, Molly, six months earlier. The family decides to go to France to recover and Hannah meets a young man. Eventually she is able to move forward with her life.

Something for Joey by Richard E. Peck Young Adult
A fictionalized true story of football star John Cappelletti who made touchdowns as medicine for his younger brother Joey, who was suffering from leukemia and died in 1976.

The Stone Pony by Patricia Calvert J/F 7-9
JoBeth's older, talented sister dies, and JoBeth tries to bury her feelings of resentment and guilt by the study of a stone pony at the local museum.

A Summer to Die by Lois Lowry J/F 7-9
Thirteen-year-old Meg has a love/hate relationship with her older sister, Molly. When Molly dies, her earlier envy turns to feelings of guilt.

The Terrorist by Carolyn B. Cooney J/F 7-9
Sixteen-year-old Laura, an American living in London, puts her mourning on hold while she tries to find the person responsible for killing her 11-year-old younger brother, Billy. As time passes, she begins to feel her grief.

Toughing It by Nancy Springer J/F 7-9
Shawn Lacey (aka Tuff) is a 16 year-old boy whose 18-year-old brother, Dillon, is murdered right in front of him. "It happened like a knife cutting my life in half," says Tuff. A short book that shows how poverty and family dysfunction impact the grief process.

When I Was Older by Garrett Freymann-Weyr J/F 7-9
Sophie had plans for when she was older, until everything changed when her brother, Erhart, died. Now 15-years-old, she has changed completely. She has difficulty dealing with the normal social life of a teenager. She meets Francis, and through her friendship with him, comes to terms with the changes in herself, and life in general.

The Year Without Michael by Susan Beth Pfeffer J/F 7-9
When 14-year-old Michael disappears one day, his 16-year-old sister, Jody, tries to cope with her loss, in spite of the additional loss of friends and what the tragedy is doing to the family. Portrays the agony of not knowing, and yet presuming that the missing child has been murdered.

General Non-Fiction about Sibling Loss

Children Are Not Paper Dolls by Erin Linn Levy NF
This is a book of drawings and quotations from young bereaved siblings. They talk about their personal experiences of loss, hearing the news, what the funeral was like, how they reacted, how their families changed, their feelings of guilt and sorrow, and what helped them to heal. A good resource for bereaved siblings of all ages.

Coping With the Death of a Brother or Sister Ruth Ann Ruiz NF
The author describes the stages of grief for siblings and comments on the impact of cause of death on the grief process.

For Those Who Live: Helping Children Cope with the Death of a Brother or Sister by Kathy LaTour
This is not a long book, but it's heartfelt compassion shines through every page. Only a bereaved sibling could have written it. The book talks about what happens when you lose a sibling-the grief that doesn't match what it "should," the change in family dynamics, the struggles and the hope. Using wisdom gathered from many sources, the author helps the reader face the reality of loss.

In the Shadow of Illness by Myra Bluebond-Langner
The author has written many academic articles about siblings who grow up with a brother or sister who has a chronic disease. Like Fanos's book, Sibling Loss, this book focuses on families with a child who has cystic fibrosis, but describes issues common to all families who have a child with a chronic or fatal illness.

An Intimate Loneliness: Supporting Bereaved Parents and Siblings by Gordon Riches and Pam Dawson
This book explores how family members come to terms with the loss of a sibling. Through research, they studied how the finding of meaning and interpretation of grief affects the bereaved parents and children.

The Lone Twin: Understanding Twin Bereavement and Loss by Joan Woodward NF
This book was written by a psychotherapist in England, who explores what happens when twins are separated, especially by death. She includes a chapter on interventions for professionals.

Losing Someone You Love: When a Brother or Sister Dies Elizabeth Richter NF
True stories written by surviving siblings age 10-24. For all ages.

Recovering from the Loss of a Sibling by Katherine Fair Donnelly NF
Numerous stories from the lives of bereaved siblings. The author points out the similarities found in sibling loss, whatever the age of the bereaved.

Shadows in the Sun: The Experiences of Sibling Bereavement in Childhood by Betty Davies NF
This book describes the major research studies on childhood sibling loss, much of which was carried out by Davies, whose mother was a bereaved sibling.

Sibling Bereavement: Helping Children Cope with Loss by Ann Farrant
Reading about the experiences of others who have lost a brother or a sister helps us realize we are not alone.

Sibling Loss by Joanna H. Fanos NF
Some brothers and sisters experience the chronic illness of their sibling prior to the sibling's death. Although this is a special kind of sibling loss, many of the issues apply to all surviving siblings.

S.O.S. Sorrow of Siblings by Parents of Murdered Children
This wonderful book addresses the difficult topic of murder and how it impacts siblings. Surviving brothers and sisters tell their stories.

Straight from the Siblings: Another Look at the Rainbow by Gerald Jamplosky NF
With drawings and quotes from bereaved brothers and sisters, the editor creates a touching memorial to the love between siblings. The book brings out not only the sadness, but also the difficult feelings, such as jealousy and guilt, that trouble the survivors. Any bereaved sibling reading this book will come away feeling included in its pages. It is full of hope and appropriate for readers of all ages, even adults who lost a sibling during childhood.

Unspoken Grief; Coping with Childhood Sibling Loss by Helen Rosen
The author describes young children's reactions to the loss of a sibling. She explains how the grieving process is prolonged by prohibitions against mourning.

Memoirs and other books

Bereft: A Sister's Story by Jane Bernstein NF
When the author was 17 years old, her 21-year-old sister, Laura, was murdered. Years later, after having children of her own, the author investigates her sister's murder and begins to come to terms with her loss.

A Book of Reasons by John Vernon NF
When John Vernon's brother dies suddenly, he searches for reasons why his brother lived the way he did.

The Boy on the Green Bicycle: A Memoir by Margaret Diehl NF
A look from adulthood back into childhood when the author was 9 years old and her 14 year old brother died. She talks about the separate grief of the family members and how the loss impacted her own life.

Dancing in the Dark: A Sister Grieves by Elsie K. Neufeld and David Augsburger NF
This is the story of a sister who writes about the death of her brother in a car accident.

The End of the Twins: A Memoir of Losing a Brother by Saul Diskin Non-Fiction
Describes the period leading to the death of the author's twin brother, Martin, and their struggles to keep him alive.

Do They Have Bad Days in Heaven? Surviving the Suicide Loss of a Sibling by Michelle Linn-Gust NF
When the author was a junior in college, her sister Diane committed suicide. It completely changed her life. This book offers education about sibling grief and hope to other suicide survivors.

An Empty Chair: Living in the Wake of a Sibling's Suicide by Sara Swan Miller NF
Written following interviews with more than 30 bereaved siblings, and aided by her personal experience with her sister's suicide, the author offers hope for those left behind.

The Empty Room: Surviving the Loss of a Brother or Sister at Any Age by Elizabeth DeVita-Raeburn NF
DeVita, a science journalist, is the sister of the young boy called the "Bubble Boy". In the book, she describes how her brother Ted's life and death have affected her. She includes interviews with others who lost siblings, including myself. DeVita considers survivors, rather than academicians or researchers, to be the real experts on this subject.

The Hurry-Up Song: A Memoir of Losing My Brother by Clifford Chase NF
The author lost his brother to AIDS in 1989.

If the Spirit Moves You: Love and Life After Death by Justine Picardie NF
Written as a diary, the book describes the year in the life of the author after her sister's death from breast cancer.

In the Season of the Daisies by Tom Phelan Fiction
Sean, now a grown man, witnessed the brutal murder of his 13-year-old twin years earlier. He was driven to madness by his grief. He turns the event over and over in his mind, trying to make the ending turn out different.

The Jim and Dan Stories: A Journey of Grief and Faith by Colleen Redman
The author lost two adult brothers one month apart—a devastating loss that she dealt with by writing. The result is an inspiring book for those who have lost adult siblings.

Landscape Without Gravity: A Memoir of Grief by Barbara Lazear Ascher NF
A beautifully written tribute to her brother, who died of AIDS. There is also information here about siblings and their grief, and how strong the bond is, regardless of whether the siblings were close.

Letters to Sara: The Agony of Adult Sibling Loss by Anne McCurry NF
The author wrote letters to her sister after her death from breast cancer. The reader learns about the grief process along with the author as she searches for anything that will help her make sense of her loss.

Memories of My Sister: Dealing With Sudden Death by Linda Rener NF
The author tells her personal story of loss and then goes on to talk about grief in general and normalize it for the reader.

My Brother Peter: Murder or Suicide? Nomi Berger NF
The author was 23 when her brother died, seemingly from drug abuse. Years later, she spent time investigating what really happened to him—was it murder or suicide? This journey was necessary for her own healing.

Phoenix: A Brother's Life by J.D. Dolan NF
When his brother, John, was injured in an explosion, the author had not spoken to him in five years. He is able to reconnect with the love he felt for his brother.

Surviving a Sibling by Scott Mastley NF
This book is a personal account of his grief experience by Scott Mastley, whose brother, Chris, died after a car accident in 1994. He talks about the profound strength of the sibling relationship and about the changes in himself as a result of his loss.

Sources

Adams, D.W. & Deveau, E.J. (1987). When a brother or sister is dying of cancer: The vulnerability of the adolescent sibling. *Death Studies, 11*, 279-295.

Applebaum, D.R. & Burns, G.L. (1991). Unexpected childhood death: Posttraumatic stress disorder in surviving siblings and parents. *Journal of Clinical Child Psychology, Vol. 20*, No. 2, 114-120.

Balk, D. (1983). Effects of sibling death on teenagers. *The Journal of School Health, January 1983,* 14-18.

Balk, D.E. (1991a). Death and adolescent bereavement: current research and future directions. *Journal of Adolescent Research, Vol. 6*, No. 1, 7-27.

Batten, M. & Oltjenbruns, K.A. (1999). Adolescent sibling bereavement as a catalyst for spiritual development: A model for understanding. *Death Studies, 23*: 529-546.

Birenbaum, L.K., Robinson, M.A., Phillips, D.S., & Stewart, B.J. (1989-90). The response of children to the dying and death of a sibling. *Omega, Vol. 20(3),* 213-228.

Bluebond-Langner, M. (1989). Worlds of dying children and their well siblings. *Death Studies,13* 1-16.

Bowlby, J. (1969, 1982) *Attachment and loss. vol. I Attachment* (2nd ed.), New York: Basic Books.

Bowlby, J. (1973) *Attachment and loss. vol. II Separation: Anxiety and Anger,* New York: Basic Books.

Bowlby, J. (1980) *Attachment and loss. vol. III Loss: Sadness and depression,* New York: Basic Books.

Bowlby, J. (1988). *A secure base: Parent-child attachment and healthy human development*. New York: Basic Books.

Brabant, S. (1990). Old pain or new pain: a social psychological approach to recurrent grief. *Omega, Vol., 20(4)*, 273-279.

Davies, E. (1983). *Behavioral response of children to the death of a sibling*. Unpublished doctoral dissertation. University of Washington. Seattle, Washington.

Davies, B. (1991). Long-term outcomes of adolescent sibling bereavement. *Journal of Adolescent Research, Vol. 6*, No. 1, 7-27.

Derdyn, A.P. & Waters, D.B. (1981). Unshared loss and marital conflict. *Journal of Marital and Family Therapy*, October, 481-487.

Elizur, E. & Kaffman, M. (1983). Factors influencing the severity of childhood bereavement reactions. *American Journal of Orthopsychiatry, 53(4)*, 668-676.

Fanos, J.H. & Nickerson, B.G. (1991). Long-term effects of sibling death during adolescence. *Journal of Adolescent Research, Vol. 6, No. 1*, 70-82.

Fox, S.S. (1985). Children's anniversary reactions to the death of a family member. *Omega, Vol. 15(4)*, 291-305.

Gilbert, K. R. (1996). "We've had the same loss, why don't we have the same grief?" Loss and differential grief in families. *Death Studies, 20*, 269-283.

Gray, J. (1984). *What you feel, you can heal: A guide for enriching relationships*. Mill Valley, California: Heart Publishing.

Hogan, N.S. & DeSantis, L. (1994). Things that help and hinder adolescent sibling bereavement. *Western Journal of Nursing Research, 16(2)*, 132-153.

Hurd, R.C. (1999). Adults view their childhood bereavement experiences. *Death Studies, 23*, 17-41.

Klein, Melanie *Love, Guilt and Reparation: And Other Works 1921-1945*. New York: Simon & Schuster

Krell, R. & Rabkin, L. (1979). The effects of sibling death on the surviving child: A family perspective. *Family Process, 18,* 471-477.

Loconto, D. G. (1998). Death and dreams: a sociological approach to grieving and identity. *Omega, Vol. 37(3)*: 171-185.

Martinson, I.M. (1991). Adolescent Bereavement: Long-term responses to a siblings death from cancer. *Journal of Adolescent Research, Vol. 6, No. 1,* 54-69.

McClowry, S.G., Davies, E. B., May, K.A., Kulenkamp, E.J., & Martinson, I.M. (1987) The empty space phenomenon: The process of grief in the bereaved family, *Death Studies, 11,* 361-374.

McCown, D.E. & Pratt, C. (1985). Impact of sibling death on children's behavior. *Death Studies, 9,* 323-335.

McNeil, J.N. (1986). Communicating with surviving children. In Rando, T. (Ed.), *Parental loss of a child* (pp. 451-458). Champaign, Illinois: Research Press Company.

Oltjenbruns, K.A. (1991). Positive outcomes of adolescents' experience with grief. *Journal of Adolescent Research, Vol. 6, No.1,* 43-53.

Parkes, C.M. *Bereavement: Studies of grief in adult life.* New York: International Universities Press.

Pfost, K.S., Stevens, M.J., and Wessels, A.B. (1989). Relationship of purpose in life to grief experiences in response to the death of a significant other. *Death Studies, 13*: 371-378.

Pollock, G.H. (1978). On siblings, childhood sibling loss, and creativity. In Pollock, G.H. (1989). *The mourning-liberation process, Vol. II* (pp. 509-547). Madison, Connecticut: International Universities Press, Inc.

Rosen, H. & Cohen, H.L. (1981). Children's reactions to sibling loss. *Clinical Social Work Journal, Vol. 9, No.3*, 211-219.

Rosen, H. (1984-85). Prohibitions against mourning in childhood sibling loss. *Omega, Vol. 15 (4)*, 307-316.

Sutherland Fox, S. (1984). Children's anniversary reactions to the death of a family member. *Omega, Vol. 15 (4)*, 29-305.

Tooley, K. (1975). The choice of a surviving sibling as "scapegoat" in some cases of maternal bereavement—a case report. *Journal of Child Psychology and Psychiatry, Vol. 16*, 331-339.

Vickio, C.J. (1999). Together in spirit: Keeping our relationships alive when loved ones die. *Death Studies, 23*, 161-175.

Worden, J.W., Davies, B., & McCown, D. (1999). Comparing parent loss with sibling loss. *Death Studies, 23*, 1-15.

Zall, D.S. (1994). The long term effects of childhood bereavement: Impact on roles as mothers. *Omega, Vol. 29(3)*, 219-230.

About the Author

P. Gill White, PhD, a professional counselor in private practice in Chesterfield, Missouri, specializes in working with individuals who have experienced the loss of a sibling. She is founder and director of The Sibling Connection (www.sibling connection.net), a not-for-profit organization based in St. Louis. She has been married for thirty-five years and has two grown children.

Index

978-0-595-38513-3
0-595-38513-3

1946936

Made in the USA